# DISOBEDIENCE

Also by Alice Notley

*165 Meeting House Lane* (1971)

*Phoebe Light* (1973)

*Incidentals in the Day World* (1973)

*For Frank O'Hara's Birthday* (1976)

*Alice Ordered Me to Be Made* (1976)

*A Diamond Necklace* (1977)

*Songs for the Unborn Second Baby* (1979)

*Dr. Williams' Heiresses* (1980)

*When I Was Alive* (1980)

*How Spring Comes* (1981)

*Waltzing Matilda* (1981)

*Tell Me Again* (1982)

*Sorrento* (1984)

*Margaret & Dusty* (1985)

*Parts of a Wedding* (1986)

*At Night the States* (1988)

*From a Work in Progress* (1988)

*Homer's Art* (1990)

*To Say You* (1993)

*Selected Poems of Alice Notley* (1993)

*Close to Me and Closer . . . (The Language
        of Heaven) and Désamère* (1995)

*The Descent of Alette* (1996)

*Mysteries of Small Houses* (1998)

with Douglas Oliver
    *The Scarlet Cabinet* (1992)

# DISOBEDIENCE

BY ALICE NOTLEY

 PENGUIN POETS

PENGUIN BOOKS
Published by the Penguin Group
Penguin Putnam Inc., 375 Hudson Street,
New York, New York 10014, U.S.A.
Penguin Books Ltd, 27 Wrights Lane,
London W8 5TZ, England
Penguin Books Australia Ltd, Ringwood,
Victoria, Australia
Penguin Books Canada Ltd, 10 Alcorn Avenue,
Toronto, Ontario, Canada M4V 3B2
Penguin Books (N.Z.) Ltd, 182-190 Wairau Road,
Aukland 10, New Zealand

Penguin Books Ltd, Registered Offices:
Harmondsworth, Middlesex, England

First published in Penguin Books 2001

Page vii constitutes an extension of this copyright page.

Library of Congress Cataloging in Publication Data
Notley, Alice, 1945–
Disobedience / by Alice Notley.
p. cm.
ISBN 0-14-100229-8 (pbk. : alk. paper)
I. Title.

PS3564.O79 D57 2001
811'.54—dc21
2001045160

Set in Sabon
Designed by M. Paul

146028962

*To Doug Oliver (Will)*
*and*
*Marion Farrier (Soul)*

ACKNOWLEDGMENTS

Some of these poems have appeared in the following publications:

the magazines *Raddle Moon, deluxe rubber chicken, disturbed guillotine, Pharos, Explosive Magazine, GAS,* and *Jacket*;

in *etruscan reader VII* (with Wendy Mulford and Brian Coffey);

and in the anthologies *Moving Borders: Three Decades of Innovative Writing by Women* (ed. Mary Margaret Sloan) and *The Outlaw Bible of American Poetry* (ed. Alan Kaufman).

# CONTENTS

# FOUR SCARVES AND A LION *(JUNE 18, 1996–AUGUST 28, 1996)*

# DISOBEDIENCE

# A SCARF OF BITTER WATER

---

*(July 30–October 6, 1995)*

# CHANGE THE FORMS IN DREAMS

moved here for no reason. don't seem to be anywhere

That's better.
                    & the only
            thing American really
worth bringing is the sense
that you must accept me, exactly.
Not as your woman.

---

I had left the American poetry masons in their burntdown hall

But I moved for no reason
at least now that's the case, today
Aug of late, early on the 9th ninety-five.
three years later

---

All over the world it's been hot.

---

No persona my face a light oval

On wall (wall of writing, in cave, in my imagination)
"In haec tempora
you will lie"

Sinister crisis/crux—
make loss? (in times of loss I don't lie)

No, but . . . portend . . . footsteps
through door, to left
I left I left the U.S. (I created more loss)
beautiful English, the house falls.

---

The first sentence (of my poem) must be "I left it."

---

What is the second sentence

The form of the wave/weave comes to me in pictures
of stars swarming to be good
in their cage.
Man on métro speaks to himself
and so he can say anything he wants.
I wish I were him

always so constricted
by you, all you, the stars.
This page is not woven yet

but any wave of light is already woven
so as I tell you the past of the glassy future
I find I need a plot to show us truth,
the graph's coordinates quotidian life and
my life forgotten from sleep or
the unconscious which must rise up
wounded from the escape, dripping blood.

---

Loves in caves are love.

---

It all
I mean, the universe
it had to
it is a universe of exactness.
The god we are in is exact.

There's nothing more serious or lighter than this
above rue des Messageries

Change the heroic mode.
Oh polluted lovely and the only thing American really
worth bringing to you is the sense
that you must accept me, exactly

# WHAT'S SUPPRESSED

I dream I'm a detective a man
trying to catch a woman
I'm in a barroom with small reflector-mirrors
high in each corner.
She's in the locked back room.
I pretend to be drunk

to blend in until she comes out?
into this room of the self full
of others and mirrors.

She is the soul.

───────────────────

Always trying to find
that back room that being
is there only such a thing as brute form wherewith,
a cheap Chandleresque detection device
a man with a coat and a gun
a room with mirrors because
I can't leave your company, your approval.

I like the mirrors, their silver
small hints of the total reflectiveness,
the litup soul/self I have been
from time to time I can't remember.

───────────────────

Down at the real corner bar, no one wants
to be here in August.
                    Six men playing cards
and drinking red wine. I stare at thin
hair dyed red
of wizened woman paying

for glass of white bordeaux
she didn't drink it all, she smiles
someone in the habit of trying to be interesting
a former tart, it's horrible that I think like that.

———————————

Hypnotize self into a fantasy world
a world of caves. (Yes, I *do* this, I can.)
Sit down before a rock wall with writing on it.
Let whatever    the E's are sharp when I touch them.
That common letter. it's surface everywhere

A shadowy man in a gun-coat has come to find me.
Why do I like these caves so much?
He seems to be asking the question.
Because evidence left in them
is our subject of detection. Is what's lost
to the presumably awakened world

I'm, we're, the result or flower of suppression.
Much of one is suppressed
towards being another kind of one
other colors, petal arrangements, scents
you can only have one scent
I want to know what I've forgotten
for 50,000 years. Think of those ridiculous *déesses*
so-called Venuses, in French museums.
What do I know. It's so fatiguing to hate you men.

———————————

Define soul: I am soul

Look on the wall: Elelse . . .

———————————

I could say that the detective
becomes even more interesting older
wittier drunk a veritable piece
of characterization for you
isn't it marvelous he reads a lot

an amateur critic/philosopher
belongs to a Derridean study group (*siècle* drags on.)

———————————————————

Become more lost in caves . . .
the caves expand, enclosure dissolves
I want to go to heaven this second
I know I can't stay I've been there before
momentarily
I float alive, larger than history.

Better than history

# SUN IS VERY NEAR HOT AND BUTTOCKSLIKE

dreaming, I accompany a pharmacist named Harward—
who wants to fill a prescription—
to the Needles Pharmacy/Mortuary
a shadowy warehouse with a counter dividing the customer space from shelves
and the obscure room behind them where bodies are laid out.
People who come by often ask, "Who's on ice in the back?"
It will be I or me or one, of course, or "Soul is it Soul?" does Soul die?
Harward is curious about, peers into, the back room
detecting?
Is the Soul just a notion, a drug?

Here, in another dream, is a white
bridge from nowhere to nowhere, a lyre-like
ramp a raised graphlike line, supported by stringlike spars
gradually up, gradually down . . . "Oh Honey don't let me
walk down that poet-like staircase into the sea!"
At the bottom in shallow water is a body the death mask
of a man, a poet, *the* poet still a man. I won't care then
or will I, detective or soul. Soul cares for.

---

I've now
named the detective Hardwood.

---

In the "real," in the métro
a man scrambles charmingly
for five francs      a busker
has lost his francs he slides under seats
pops up before people unexpectedly
he dropped it somewhere collecting coins
after his guitar performance, which I missed.
He has a female assistant.
I exit into hot empty—

no one even at—Concorde
I'm a poet so I go buy a book.

———————————

Caves. Enter the room with the writing on the wall
sometimes all the people are there and not up above "in life"
they crowd round me while I examine the letters
"ELF the gasman pleasantly wants your world."

I enter a further room. I look so young
an owl—symbol of a certain dead soldier—
has come to scourge me for my untroubled appearance
lines sink immediately into my face and this is I . . .
the detective, will he like
such an aging soul's face?

———————————

Descend farther into a lower room
several of us sit on the floor, women in shrouds or serapes
and the white sulphurous owl not corny is there.
We sense the fire, the sickening smell of war—
"When you stab a man to death there's a terrible smell!"—
all over the real world while the soul tries to claim itself.

All the detectives take drugs—Chirac, write your own
prescription and fill it

if Hardwood's more sensitive than you, a sweet guy
with a carved wooden gun
or bronze one with silver trimmings
a soulful gun, should I stand by him?

What would you have done in World War II they always say,
as if the past solved anything, rather than caused it.

———————————

Later dreaming pleasantly that I was that dead poet
asleep and dreaming.

Still later,
in cave:

Touch carved E finger bleeds.

Then, outside the cave, I hurry alongside a vaporous lake.
Dante, a cartoon Dante is here, in Dante clothes
face featureless.

How large to have a white dead face like
the moon and hover above others. Oh help me
No you don't need help

Who did I ask who answered it wasn't Dante.

Don't, don't be Dante. But don't, don't be an E.

———————————————

Each poem quivers as I do and then flows forwards

# I SUPPOSE THIS IS ALL A LEFTHAND PATH

Detective Hardwood looks like Batman this morning
pouty cupidy mouth
and a lot of black sculptural clanking
the statuary in my mortuary,
the Masonic Hall having burned again in dreams
but everyone still keeps skipping towards it
it's a hollow a round shell
my life as the shape of the ways I've been fucked
by prevailing thought & practice
all the conscious and unconscious sexisms
selfishnesses affluences assumptions suppressions in drift

GET RID OF ALL CONTROLS—is what the Soul keeps screaming.

————————————————

I look up someone grins
you're a bloody feral wolf-face I like you.

————————————————

I sleep-walked in a dream to a man's apartment—
a man I'm doing business with—
I forgot, but how could I? how I'd gotten there,
and when I die will I remember all such forgotten things?

GET RID OF THE CONTROLS
                              I want to
remember now.

I apologized to the man for not adhering to office hours
it was four a.m. Office hours *are* better he said.

Don't arrive anywhere in your sleep
don't mix up night and day
soul and detective. No.

There must be so much to reclaim
because I'm so limited

---

this.
They broke your day
they fought it you
forgot how advantageous
to be fit with god and not see eye
you forgot gold sun brilliant
in this story
go in conscious.

---

That queen that Assyrian woman
was so cruel and that never
occurred to her . . . but

those eyes saw raw smells and gods everywhere dusty

this dust I was truly assembled from
at least as you, we are communally
such.

If you say you'll hurt me, do you
really mean me

*I* can't be, can I, hurt?

---

"Hut Sut Tut Mut there's gonna be a wedding"
I dream that's a song. Wake up with, in my head,
"They say don't go
on Wolverton Moun-tain" ("Her tender lips/are sweeter than hone-y")

---

Later.
I have a drop of blood on a front tooth
I kind of don't mind—

This is the list of what we've done:

> It was different structure we killed it
> put beasts in the refrigerator
> and that was almost as bad as my own enslavement.
> Then I saw Christ's blood pumped into a rejuvenating mummy.
> This great sickness we're part of apple clot
> and can you really chew it detective
> Oh sure I can, I'm Robert Mitch-ham.

————————————————

you've broke your own sto

I'm sort of hysterical

the E is it for hope, cutting

the E might be for Hope

Nope

and bloody, the bloodiest is Hope.

Where are the E's of exactness?

E is my middle name

## WHERE *IS* THE BABYLONIAN METER WITH ITS LOVELY CAESURA?


"biggest problem in the world now is its unity"

. . . lovely? Internet, business, the English language, no nature
beautiful . . . you're in charge, you member you
of the elite educated class it's all up to what
you choose to buy—the job you have
(what nearly lost culture
are you fucking over today? . . . )

And I assisting in this gruesome unification
by emigrating from America to France.

———————————————

Perhaps Hardwood will take me on a tour of
Our Loss—later?
The soul's confidante as vital to her as I am to you dear.

———————————————

A smell of sun-baked earth water origanum and also
a clove-scented flower

That tree with crimson blossoms gold-centered
almost opened up what memory center in me?
But it won't come.
It was some sort of happiness.
The happiness itself oozed up materially.

———————————————

Where is the story the path through
I want a unity for it—because I,
        I am unified exactly
the human world is unified in a different way . . .
        accidentally,
by technology and aggression.

The detective's standing in the middle
of this giant cavern again, in his giant giant coat and big
hat
        "Let's find something," he says
        I follow the swish of his cloth
this room is white. (I think he is will)
A tiny theater a play on the floor the size of a fire in a fireplace
white-yellow-red figures, the red blossoms from the Jardin "blooming"
I remember seeing them in this future that's why they were so poignant.

The reason it's, whatever, is even more in memory:
your job's constantly to make your life "Why?"
as a person not a poet "Why?"
That's Soul asking and Hardwood thinks he knows
"Because otherwise there isn't time to"
But it doesn't have to get made I say, does an owl make
her life on reflection? "She doesn't have to she can fly
flight is like thought Who's speaking Soul pushes Hardwood away He's
doing all the thinking No who's thinking.

Down in caves another time, down a musée-like cavern
walls of blank rock behind panes of glass
this is supposed to be the tour of our loss
but we've forgotten, now, what animals looked like
can't see our loss.

In the exact world
to make ends meet draw an arrow
a positron moving backwards in time
grasps yesterday quickly before dying.

Down into there into real black

Do you need Microsoft Windows

juicy melancholy
remember the first time I
inhaled smog beneath a tangerine sun (I had
a friend now dead who loved that experience.)

Turn on a light, look at wall—
Mitch-ham is here—there's
a column of tiny words
"settle in setback for now
subatomically going backwards
the memory of the puzzle is
to gather a step going forward
I was your anti-particle
in this lightly dualist
world, where Bill Gates you particle
the future, because the immediate past
is rather weak-souled and so you
like a hawk flying to no freedom
on a long string.
(Change immediate past.)"

I need those windows says a new Dante
Oh, great.

*"Louis Blanc. Il est blanc."* Always.

A woman stealing thistles was what I saw last week
in the alpine garden of the Jardin des Plantes
when I was so exquisitely hot

# CIRCORPSE

there's really only one, but there's hardly any interest
if there aren't two or more:
That's why I keep on letting Hardwood detect me.

_____

No one cares if the world is a big fat America
as long as we've got our windows windows windows.
(Change immediate past)

Suddenly everyone says
they care and they have been caring, that would be an example
of changing the past in order to go forward
"Well that wasn't what I did because I didn't have a motive yet.
I was waiting for disaster itself."
(Who's speaking?)

"I wanted to get lost inside I would die, going in through wind—
so imagined have I become
that I will never die
in fact have never been . . . "
(Who's speaking?)

_____

Trying to find or be a dark woman. the soul I am.

Caves now enter along thin stream through cracked rock
a waterfall and flowers, smell of moist rock turn
down into caverns (like Mitchell's Caverns     lost secrets of
        the Chemahuevi)

a ranger/guide is with us . . .

"Many branches of the caves
are beyond both dogooders and smartasses," he says,

"haunted therefore by Dante-like creeps.
If you want to find a woman here she isn't 'good' either."

––––––––––––––––––––

Another bomb exploded in Paris a few days ago,
left in a trashcan at the Arc de Triomphe
eighteen people including some little kids injured.
This is probably a crime motivated by religion
The suspect group has especially targeted women, in Algeria . . .
as dispensable commodity prone to be filthy
dark as a dudgeon (I wrote that last word by accident.)

So there was a bomb scare yesterday at Métro Cadet
someone left a blank gray package on our train
we were ordered off panicking.
What does that have to do
with a big fat America?
Plenty.

––––––––––––––––––––

The entrance to the caves
is pinpointed by graph lines this morning
when I enter it's spooky dark.
The ranger's here again

Don't misunderstand good, he says,
You would, being disinterestedly good, transcend it.
Where's old Hardwood now, that stick . . .
See via such banality as a detective/actor? No
The figure Dante *could* absorb old Hardwood
But no you're not worthy of such an asshole as Dante
for your confidante or guide or foil,
people might get offended . . .
presumption, pre-emption.
Dante's gonna get lost. I know I'll choose
Hardwood/Mitch-ham.

––––––––––––––––––––

Priority to some creatures?
As I outfoxed some others

I'm sitting on the same old flower sheet
in my same old leopard-spotted lounge-dress;
having dreamed last night that Michael J. Fox
chose to wear his animal suit, in a musical theatrical production
on top of buildings in New York City
where many full bins were—I suppose they were my "beens."

———————————————

Am I seriously Soul?

When time goes away I don't care about
me (him or me)
The phone rang; we're meeting at 1:30.
What do I use my personality for? Humor was there from the beginning . . . And
the behavior of certain elementary particles seems rather humor-filled;
certainly unpredictable. There are equations that 'cover' this unpredictability.
The relation of I, soul, to particle: I think I am its field of familiar
the non-niggling corpus
playing, like a photon, myself: watch me I'll behave another way from usual.
Deeper, under the fox costume,
I'm more than I say in time
but time's less exact than I am.
Want to be with just about anyone who'll let me talk too.
Hardwood yaps at me
"How can you catch the bad guys if you like them?"
I say, "I only want to yell
at them."

———————————————

I've found a dark woman, a chicana
she's just let another man enter
the ancient, former Needles Auto Supply
after attention, flirtation, on her part. She sees that I'm jealous—
of those attentions or of her?
Was he my man? this is complicated;
'We'll get you some,' she seems to say, and hugs me
and her friend, a small black girl braids sticking out, hugs me
then I'm placed on the belly of a fat sexless man
lying on his back on the ground, and bounced up and down.

She speaks but I know she is me:
mouths words—what are they—and smiles:
"Am I ready to be different now, in a world of bloody souls?"
Am I ready for the world of you, slippery
you whom I may never understand

# HELP ME CORPUS SAGRADA

to be as tough as mean as Akhmatova
as durable as her last tooth.
In my dream, an old crone
she's finally gassed to death by a dentist
who wants to extract her one huge
tooth and analyze it.

---

Last night a Martiniquaise, tall woman a "danseuse"
is barred from the Polly Magoo.
She's always paid her bills she says so she obviously hasn't
she never picks up men, for the past ten years has masturbated
that can't be true either
and she's exultant.

---

Hardwood is dying to tell me his life story
says he's tough too.

---

Enter the caves to find out what's suppressed
is that a specious project more E's.

This angel's wings are limp ribbons
her body floats circorpse, the surrounding natural love
'Gone to the grave door, you stupid dress
the grave door of the future.'
Spoken by her or Hardwood?

My insolent features, young, long suppressed
swim in the face of my future concern
for a fucked-up world: could only be a jerk when young.

Could I once have lived to be so wrong? Yes.

I must be pretending to be someone:
have you all been making me pretend
along my whole life of E     A-lice Elizabeth

Go to the grave door, dress
and pretend that the future will be more, more of this . . . procrastination
a woman walks to a gravestone covered
with E's. Evolution Forever, it says
she opens a door

and enter there's light down here
and more descent of course.

_____

I don't want to be like.
My old hair floods you with cars in it lice,
kneel down and listen to the ground:
"We will be in the new deluge,
we the wake of the former flood.
And there is an island in Sumer
where the inhabitants are descended from people
from before the flood."

_____

The sentence:

You will always be in others' arms
                                    and
the horror of society
                    is its friendship, most certainly
In order to help or love you must be like.

Flies' asses. What's that French expression?
A fucker of flies up the ass: a stickler for detail.

_____

Hardwood first saw the light
in a birth canal in the Southwest
flies swarmed
so he could grow up to be like details.

I still like him anyway
I have to

And Lady, I have to like you too.

------

Child-abandoning home-wrecker Anna A
Forgot about her along the way.

And so left holding the fishbowl?
that contains the tiny ones, the usual the men
gesticulating in the mid-night of de-struction.
Their vicious fleas bite my hand and cause blood to flow
purple and foamy
but I'm still glad to be alive
not dead like Anna,
though some of the dentist's gas almost reached me.

------

These lacunae are most great, most restful.

Do I really want to fill them in with suppressions?

------

The Choros of the future howls quietly.

------

"I'd see her number if you'd see her really,"
Inspector Hardwood says
(is that the dark woman I am)

# THE ISLANDERS REMEMBER THAT THERE ARE NO WOMEN AND NO MEN

in the antediluvian island
in the primordial swamp
Hardwood was already my friend

The porcelain basin of memory is black
I spit down it brushing my feral tooth.

---

'A double? oh really badly'

I have a
double a self I can't stand

I was discovered by primordial Columbus
and became his land?
Cliché says Hardwood.

---

Wanting the real
and as a dream is a dream
I try to remember something:
the trees at Blythe
at night, going home
inside the steel cab of a pickup,
road lined with athol trees. salty, drab.
Home gone to feels empty
a little shakily and that's
more like a dream than a memory.

No I want real and dreamed to be fused into the real
rip off this shroud of division of my poem from my life.

I am a reflex an E for effort
(what I can't stand)—

equal to a shroudperson.

Eating eels near the Loire I learn to slither
not between poles but being the one pole the river.

Now that I've visited an *étang*
I always had visited one—
I knew these swamps when the stars.
An island of Sumer, no dead other
dark woman or enemy-maker.

Become
this:

I haven't known such
efflorescence    like the gold dust and red laughing tree
I was trying to remember before
what is exact here an E for example
or my tooth chattering, almost, with excitement
        because first it happens
        and then you make it your life,
                                this,
that when we were at the swamp on Sunday
it wasn't the swamp till yesterday
so I go back sometime before the swamp
to make the swamp happen more exactly,
to a night of stars after eels were eaten
out of such a night, with the town stretched out
a flotilla with trees and above, the old castle
out of that modern and crumbling past
create something older and more original
and so in this one windy swamp (the next day)
become, and in company, saltier, tangier

a taste from the future of my union
when I'll have been here.

---

ugly Paris

---

Hardshroud I mean Hardwood
says of course the city is my shroud,
if you unwrap it Babylon ugly
Ninevah, Ur ugly
it's so ugly to be here
with salt on my tongue, of dying into
a worse future I'm leaving
that you can't change.

---

I've been there now a very sharp experience
on an island of Sumer where I had no impatience with Hardwood
that frog don't jump
don't jump away.

Our opposable thumbs will be opposable shrouds
and one will then pretend it's been made equal
to the other, the left to the right

This poem is a lefthand path

It's about me, exactly

I'm diminished by anyone's refusal to be equal.

So tied up and gagged, still, I'm a view of a body on the floor
feet first so you can see that I'm wearing jeans.

How will I know when I'm untied
(Déjà-vu, saying that)

## RED FISH

but I've changed something . . .

_____

What's changed,
I've cleaned some rooms. Ugh in one
dream a woman finds a large
banana-like turd with a slick skin.
As I flush it it speaks in a high-
pitched male voice, vindictively,
"You won't have no Momma!"

_____

In order for there to be    one fixed quality
another quality must    remain fluid
between its    two    possibilities
in these    electron box    experiments.

I am fixed though not a quality when nothing else is fixed.

_____

Caves. Going down to beautiful words descending to rosettes
I want to follow
a delightful path.
Inside this petalled swamp or Sumer
a lotus's wedge perforated
through which are emitted perfections of transient sensations . . .
scents, tastes, flourishes on warm temperatures—
everything I've ever wanted.

I show the red blossom to others
but after August the island of summer we change
we live in Europe where
all now work as hard as Americans.

The French call
homelessness, unemployment *'l'exclusion.'*

---

Who do you exclude he says

and I was just thinking 'It's better to let her squirm first.'

Where are those heights?

Dante has turned
his familiar ass to me that peculiar sun

and yet I feel clean.

---

Oh yes some arts are much higher

At the top of my waterfall I calmly let go
pronounceable E torrent

I'll show you, Dante Hardone! . . .

and show you the more usual misery, of which you said nothing.

---

Dante and Hardon I mean Hardwood
are different except for occasionally,
randomly, in the hard and soft electron box
of these times' preoccupations.

---

Inside this arcade of Parisian India
there is first a barefoot alcoholic
filth on feet, and the bottle, green I think.
People call us to eat here but, actually,
it's too expensive . . .
(not a dream). So many men with dirty feet
try to sleep on the métro, try to sleep through

their own smell.
That scent that temperature, August
inside, that I can appreciate I think
if I can only be I. So much I wouldn't 'mind';
to mind such smells is to think in bonds.

---

This story without bandages
will take place, my left hand
is unwrapped.

Hardwood wants to know
can a turd be a mother
Not if it's a man, I say.
That turd lied when he implied
he was my Momma.
The Turd Man, Hardwood says, not me or Dante
Of course not, I say, reassuringly.

---

Down in the gentle caves
sit on sand a river's near and air from the outside.
Who is Hardwood has willed me this far,
sometimes he's soft because    I am now dark.

The lines on the river form words only the river can read
this is the I the Loire prehistoric
I let my arms get dark as I slept while I worked
carrying scum from tree-site to sandbar
depositing it in banks for inspection and approval.

I is for *ire* to go; remaining stable that way
so far,
soft, so far; Hardwood floats, happy scum

# ENUMA ELISH

caves.
Is there a woman painted on the wall?
by a man his stylization . . .
'I can't like it'
let wind blow more words in, drift of a stone bed.

---

I saw *your* people, mine
seemed less well-defined
yours all dressed in the same rags
but no not mine.

---

Maybe even before the flood
in the backwards city      cubist
her dark face becomes blocks and chunks
she is being formed from a description
or possibility of human making.

---

I saw Mitch-ham old and drunk, formed of his cubes for my eye.
When I wasn't supposed to be looking he
dissolved into a puddle of mirror mercury.

---

The high sheriff of anyone is choice.
Will you choose cubes or not

I don't want a choice at all I want fundament

stop thinking
float script E's so pretty
enuma elish

riding the first flood itself, of bitter chaotic water
(and what a tangy aftertaste)

not the second flood god-sent but the first flood a god itself.

------

It's always Mitch-ham himself
down in these caves.
A sort of light says the words,
'you are not   choice,' or is it
'chair.' The chair you sit in an
illusion that a person can matter.
No person matters
unless humans choose a mattering style
so we choose it in various ways all over creation . . .
but, before
I didn't
*choose* or *matter*, nothing was so *important*.
One wasn't so urgently ready
to excel or kill or write—
was one just bored?

Is this the same old origination shit myth and apple?
'I am origi' a voice says to me
in a real dream
'She saw a voice; she saved her; sea of faces.'

------

*Enuma elish la nabu shamamu* . . .
the caesura comes after *elish*.
A-lice Elishabeth Caesar.
'When there was no heaven, no earth, no height, no depth, no name . . .'
wasn't I there partaking how lovely with you.

------

Underground river is what
chaos, Tiamat, becomes.
I follow her stream through caves
sit down beside a pool.
My reflection is

'ashes' I want to say—why?
For I see I forthright and youthful.

—————————————————

E's and A's skim across the water ashes
letters we've never needed?
spelling words like 'heart' and 'bear' (endure)—
or 'textual' 'intellect'—
Asking me to put up with it.
I must accept others' superpositions
Well I don't.

—————————————————

face form feral familiar flush

—————————————————

Mitch Hardapple, you who are my
will, take my hand . . .

letters and words circling in a wind

An E has fallen on my cheek like an insect.

—————————————————

A you who isn't Mitch or "real."
You are watching me? Who are you?
This is that crystalline
substance or spirit—I mean I feel it substantially
within and without
is it an I or a You?
Overmore.

(The vowels are different in her or his
language, here
in France—
this substance the same.)

There is
what knows me
what is it

# THE FOREST/SWAMP/GORGE/ALP HOTEL

before the ancient church and before the Roman amphitheater
after the time perhaps when Mount Ventoux upthrust
sitting in 8:40 a.m. sunlight blast over right shoulder
in anticipation of when wild forms have mostly
receded south from Orange, and there will be rioting in Papeete
over nuclear tests in the Pacific
I remember that I will release myself as chemicals to the air
and earth at death and that is all that ever happens?
except in the human imagination . . . Oh, sure.

This morning's thought will be
superseded by ruins.

———————————————

Mitch wants to be in a Euromovie
Outdated in the States, no American would go, I say.
The American public wants itself
the American poet wants only itself worldwide
only an American, only an American.

———————————————

The mindful electrons . . .
and in my speaking
I wasn't spoken by another's mind at all.
Nor did I talk for you, as you, like you.

The waters of Tiamat are very close.
Because I blew up the car that brought me to France
two nights ago, in a dream.

———————————————

Sun lights those chairs sapphire across square
no one matters
but anyone's mind is everything
even behind stony words and idiot placards.

In the poeto successo movie
(Tiamat the dragon just a snake)
remake the world, radically, some more, like everyone else.

Do I want
no effect on it now.

———————————————

Near more ruined theaters, more plots of fathers . . .
Her hair's becoming naturally dyed red by now.

This landscape belongs to no country.

———————————————

Convincing red-haired her to stay
with someone—his son—
who has another wife too,
it's the father, who can convince
anyone of anything:

look at them convincing you still
philosophy, science, literature—
everyone's convictions come from them;
in consequence a harping feminism . . .
and this is my old hat. But it's only a few years old
their old hat is thousands.

———————————————

Sheer gorge hell and cars
teetering around its narrow rim
everyone trying to be smart that the future
be ruins of your ass, worshipped
under floodlights by tourists—

smart things do look better broken.
Ruined art looks better, ruined ideas,
the parts you most loved gone—
the gloss and color, illusion
of dominance, I'm glad
that only two words of mine might remain.

We never made it to Daddy Cézanne's
château. Good.

I love, love bitter waters.

Notre Dame du Roc on top of the precipice
Tiamat rushes in
into the vale all broody
'I don't want your peace your things
your precious little lyings
the sentiments of your intellect, sayings of position—'
'That ain't love,' says Hardwood
'Is too,' I say.

Stop trying to make something.

A worse person may be better

clear through her waves.

Dream briefly I'm at some sort of heroin score . . .

pool of menstrual blood in front of a statue

# LANA TURNER AT VERSAILLES

the problem is that I'm wearing a dress
(I walk downtown from Morningside Heights
feeling depressed. I'm wearing a dress.)

I have a new small tape recorder
but the even newer model, *flat* and *square*
requires a trip to a Grand Magasin
to sign up for solfeg' or is it perfect pitch . . .
then I can have the tape recorder *cheap*
210 francs, if I sign up for the course.

---

My friend had a book of jewelry (pouches
attached to pages, and filled with beautiful necklaces)
but I had myself, the turquoise and silver
Indian ring I'd worn when I was four
was on my finger—no longer suppressed—
it doesn't matter now if I'm wearing a dress.

---

Who are you, real, whom I won't name
disturbing my cave with your railing

you're jealous of my clarity, my fun and bossiness

a pretty embroidery thrown over this Parisian fucking rain
this grey of the Lord's Work.

You're just one of the poetry Masons.

---

In my exactitude down here today
I'm smeared with dark paint and have my hair in waves
the regular kind an aunt used to make with metal clamps—

you can't escape style, cubes or waves.
'Dark Lady' says Hardmitch so boring
surrounded by people, the rest of the conversation . . .

'Are you the Masons?' 'We're more poetry Masons
following you
to make you behave'

Dark woman speaks, it's I,
automatic almost autonomic:
". . . not too many to feed. not even now
don't behave, feed them."

———————————————

## LANA TURNER AT VERSAILLES

as the entrance to Paris
"Shall we go on to Fame?" she says,
and answers "Yes"
I'm darker than she is but do wear that dress

and I got up
and I turned . . .
Fame is just E, like evanescent

Oh Mitch-ham let's e-mote
I, too, as common as an E, am evincing
original self under new needlework.

———————————————

My daytime self still following me
as my autumn fellows . . .

Lana Turner, don't speak now.
"But am I not equal to Dante," she says,
"as non-entity dead,
at this point?"

Mitch-ham's arm around my waist . . .

A person is exact because she's packed
a package
of characteristics
light, vegetation, the rocks
of hope, the mountains of unconscious permanence.

---

This week is so distracting
everyone wants a piece of mine

say 'Enuma elish' at each bomb scare.
We regret to inform you Mesdames and Messieurs
that métro service is interrupted
because of a suspicious package at Palais Royale.

---

A darkness immense, and dragged by a human head
in an Egyptian coif, will cover the earth
when I'm dead?

There is a human or mindlike "thing"
                                        throughout the stars
those E's—not to be read but can be said.

---

To say death is to know, to marry your death
I do.
But one doesn't have to

"YOU"

meanwhile, the beaches
of the East Coast of the U.S.
are likely to disappear in the remainder of my lifetime.

_____

Then why am I in these paleolithic
caves? touch a deer
I already don't remember
decorated so long ago
tallow combed into my hair
Have I ever liked a time?

They're charming the herds, out of love
the same way you'd write a love poem
drawing the deer on the wall, in longing, of course.

_____

Now I'm sitting in the dirt, at a different campfire
in my best black wool skirt, and beaded sweater

they're going to help me be darker
approach me with the paint that will make me "free."

Hardwill will be initiated too
they've shredded his trenchcoat
and sewn it back together in patchwork—
looks like Robinson Crusoe, reconstituted will.

Wake up, he says
let's wake up and be modern and normal—

The world isn't normal, I say, it's melting and flooding
desiccating, blowing in typhoons.

_____

"It's been 129 degrees every day this week," my mother
of the weather, in Needles, California, August, 1995.

---

What's a "lovely" complaint

not in this age.

You are not really exact
you were never a deer
you said that you were a victim
and hungry, when you had possessions:
your house, your car, your flag,
your hunger.

---

Who is this "you?"

animal on the wall

There is a you that all try to make me
make me or you,
a spangled airy fabric that won't come to form
for love or hate
—that terrifying giant of an antlered
deer, in the Musée now . . .
who are you?

---

Who are you?

As I become darker I think I find out

(don't make anything, rid of controls, dark)

I'll steal out into the night to watch animals.
Because I've never ever seen them.

A fox, smaller than I thought.
I later find it mangled, bloodied.
and that cry    the scream of something
            crazed, not evil.
It's in pain, it might be myself
            or a relative.

---

I see her she's me holding hands to her ears
not to hear her own screaming.
What's going on. Because she isn't, isn't an animal
dark enough to disappear or see.
Now she holds a bowl in each hand
casts away the contents of one, and sets it down
the right-handed one. Drinks the liquid in the other.
There's a drop of blood in my soup
it's the blood of You.

---

Tell me what to write now (I, the hand, ask
the one in the forest, in me, in Paris, in September—)

She grabs the pen jerkily.

Bitterness in chunks. Of course I'm not. anyone.
but I am bitter, because
(pokes at earth with fingers of right hand)
. . . find vicious circle "Maria"
I want a weakness . . .
violently got—
split open to stars. So I can die, be whole.
I cut it.

---

Because being    isn't just    gentle.

I'm
gentle, Hardwood avers.
I never wanted to see you like this
amid dangerous requiems.

I'm worth three times as much, I say,
but if I say that I only have worth
 . . . refuse to be overintentional, do you agree with me Hardware?

## ". . . I THOUGHT SHE WAS GOING TO BE A GHOST STORY"

I looked at my legs and they were much
hairier than I'd ever noticed
was it something about a new light?
Also I had hair on my back
which I could see.

---

Creepily a ghost
wants me for his own
when I'm dead—

Climbing down to floor of cavern
wince when my foot touches rock floor—
a tear in my real Alice eye.

---

I'm Hardwood himself now
filling a great coat—
why do the hungry dead want her?
Too *per*sonal—spit out the Per—
what is too personal, oh silly poets
their rules puerile dicta
when ghosts are alive in the forest
who want a Dante to speak to their
pain, window to see through
flaws are to see through, wounds are, and
the personal.
So ghosts pluck at others' reason
pieces of which might free them,
being trapped in our personal evils
your own creepiness, Mr. or Ms., poet
of the spotless
impersonal word.

Walk in trenchcoat into vast cavern
tiny, tiny-coated

I'm looking for ghosts or looking
for her, A-lice in the dark.

---

The Detective cries because he has to be strong
Mitch-ham downing fierce bourbon tears

yeah I've heard of my significance
you could also have called it 'use':
careers
based on the new
pedestrian interpretations
of dickheads under the stars . . .
postmodern critic approaches dick
company cliché career shears in hand.

---

So this is the forest

why are you doing this this way
writing this poem this way
I can't help it now . . .

---

Left: primary sense weak, worthless.
The Controls keep you right-handed,
to work them; left, as abandoned: They
leave me, I mean as soon as
I'm absolutely used up genre.

What is the weakest way to go . . . so
I follow
I'm following a Black Doll, almost a cliché
both of us but I
have to see her, follow soul

I am the form of myself but much more.

---

(Pouring rain in Paris)

I, Alice, dreamed my brother was a ghost
a young long-haired skinny adolescent.
I rush toward him but then he says
'I want you, I need you, I love you; I'll have
you when you die . . .' I try to tell him
he doesn't mean that.

I'm ashamed of the dream's sexuality:
I think it stands for the power of his death over me.

---

We *must* leave the land of the White Giant—
whose skin isn't green beans but white beans,
*haricots beurre.*

---

So, suffer. So, reason speaks. The West the white
West is an
incestuous ancestral tangle of warriors' (brother
a warrior) honor—
will eat your death; as critics assume
your poem into their competition.

Follow the dark doll, free the ghosts, suffer dissolution
of a culture in yourself, and find You.

I, Hardwood, use my flawed form to do this:
temper, disdain, melodrama, misanthropy
violence
(who's more violent, her or me?)

# JUST UNDER SKIN OF LEFT LEG

a dark woman, Camelia Luna
who has Anna Akhmatova's nose
welcomes me to her basement floor dwelling—
I'll help her carry her dead father
I tie him to myself, by the neck . . .
"He must be heavy," she says. He
wakes up and mutters unmemorably.

We called Camelia Cammy (pronounced
Commy) when I was a kid

Virginia my former therapist called me "loony"
"loony poet"—"You were this loony poet."

———————————————

Heavy with the season. Don't want to give myself
to a new cycle of work and socializing.
Say something pretty: "Dorior, more golden than a door."

Anyone gets tired of carrying fathers.
In my dream Cammy's father
had been a Mafia don. She answered the door
in a blue tulle dress.

———————————————

"This poem needs your love."
An American might say that
how disgusting
Love an American: "they just *love* us."
Get some Housing Projects; listen to Rap in them;
turn rightwing electing a maskface in a nice suit;
explode some nuclear bombs.
Americans come to Paris to find out they're Americans
how interesting for them; I mean us

tired of carrying that, carrying that weight
around my neck, who the fuck is this man?
depicted as the weight of your life, can
he be the brunt the cruelty
of that? Yes *I* carry him, carry him . . .

---

Out in the forest with an empty pickle jar
waiting to catch a pickle, no a pygmy owl, or
*something like that!*
                if way beneath
my surface, I can find only a diatribe,
shouldn't you listen? Way . . . way below—
where the *real* story must be.

---

Marguerite Yourcenar said
she wouldn't be in a book of women
collection of women's writings because
only women would read it, and
they already knew they were angry—
        And
anger, she said, is one, one person
a little personal sputter.
But that's that kind of anger, Marguerite—
        what about
an anger like Dante's, a whole leaden sky
a church-charged orthodox anger,
creating, in Amer-lingo, a norm for the Great?
That's *not* so bad, to damn in perpetuity,
if you're Great?
Well, she says,
it's certainly not trivial.

---

I can't seem to get down into the caves
and the lovely pleasures of the pursuit of Soul
by Will. What will happen, will I ever find me
in such a way that I'll change, off the page?

I know where Dante might be—
tied round my, Camelia Luna's neck.
"What did he say when he spoke?"
Who cares?
The weight round my neck should die.

'Hi, Mitch.' 'Hi.
Catch anything in that jar?'
'A dead man's ass disguised as light.'

'Aren't you being hard on D? He's like me'
'And me—'

First to the left, then to the right—

No, left, all the way to the left
Take it as far as you can.

Walking with my toes curled as if I were in orgasm;
now look up at the strange sky above soft trees.

I don't want to create any meaning;
I want to kill it . . .
You made meaning; I'm
trying to make life stand still,
long enough so I can exist.
I, truly, am speaking

# "HAVE MADE EARTH AS THE MIRROR OF HEAVEN"

my name is Alice Elizabeth, so am I
Allie Sheedy of the movie *Short Circuits* thus angry
or Elizabeth McGovern self-controlled?
This question is posited
on a television screen where I can't quite identify
the actress shown—which is she?

I am Allie and I will continue to rant.

_____

My voice rises in real life often—
because I am 'passionate' . . . that's
a convenient word.

_____

I'm still in the forest, darkening
wishing I were 'nicer.'

Hardwood says, You should stand up soon
I'll help you
I say, I have cramps
I say, I'm using my period, to get pissed off and to Know.

_____

I dreamed, last night, about an immense Dead Seal
below the surface of the water in a harbor

pull the curtain down.
For months you would not break the spell
for eternities you have not done so, citing economic
exigencies; the whole thing is a mess.
I might rather be dead
than doing what it takes to keep the seal under water
whale-sized

E is for seal. For spell. For suppression.

---

To take part in you is to die
is why one dies
Have I said this before?

---

I am Alp the Dizzy.

---

The dead seal isn't a person, it's poetry the seal
the hallmark
of selfhood, dead grotesquely large and richly hardening.

"Hardwood it was someone like you
you drowned the seal"

"No I'm making both you and it 'hard.' "

---

And I'm still in the forest.

---

And I'm still in the forest

Money's more the real live poetry
abstract symbolic imaginary
trade your life for it and trade it for your life
so you'll have something 'to do'

Sink the whale
and sleep all day in the real world, up and functioning
more fully imagined and dreamed, in society's
than in your own, imagination?

I'm standing
I'm standing up Hard
I keep being Hardwood myself, dark and hard.

Initiating a new 'broken symmetry' (spinning to the
Left, like a newborn neutrino)
so that we can have a new consciousness . . .
am I doing that? Yes I think so.

---

The forest contains a French restaurant
every meter or so . . .
difficult to fast in this dream vision.
We're a very unpopular group today
We've shot off another great bomb
and we've shot down a terrorist,
an Arab, young, before
we even found out what he "knew."

---

Tell me something beautiful, bitter
because we are somehow bitter, forever,
a taste included in origin, in love, in you.
So I don't have to be cloyed.

　. . . soul's waters are reticent
sly swamps.
　　　　　It had nothing in it,
that swamp; because I didn't know how to look for
the parts of its obvious whole—death is
minute, flavorful parts—which are said to spin
as I'm said to walk, moving while else
mostly unconscious of that.

---

In the new consciousness

# LEFT SIDE LIBERATION FROM E

in the left where I was abandoned,
ritually, in a forest, the left side of my
self was pulled further
into an inky thicket, I stood in
Your flaw.

_____

In the flaw you have defined
as power and force, instead of as love:
gravity, electricity, charm.
Fair . . .
but not brilliant.

                    In the flaw if I
make my other hand work,
the love between
the two hands will be balanced.

I don't. You won't let me

The powerful right hand loves skills
the left hand dreams (it's dreaming
this poem.)

_____

These dreams are more powerful than bombs
because they don't have to move to affect me—

You, you asked for a bomb-maker
a righthand kind of scientist, or a
geneticist to make us . . . not ambidextrous but
square    enough    to be understood    by you.

I stand in your flaw and choose
I've my left hand weak
it isn't love's hand at all
it's the hand of . . . *unknow it*

(written with
left hand)

that's death but if you
unknow now
left hand:) *in your fate*

you can . . . not "balance"
but be equal to
(left hand:) *the life.*

---

there's a wind through my sweater
not saying;
it's even left of the famous heart

I have to     love your flaw
but, to the left, is so awesome
and you won't even go with me

(left hand:) *beyond love.*

---

That's the way it is.

---

I'm writing near rational
soberest Mitch-ham now.

You have no respect for anyone else
while you're writing, he says to me.

No I don't. And that's correct, the correct way to be.

E

others in the caves a strange
entity there a wide sentient
absence     E for that entity.

E has arms, gesticulates apparently speaking
no one can hear him. It's not that he's mute
it's that he's . . . epi . . . epi . . .
epidural     but not epiphanic.
Language uninhabited,
just a quick
fix. a surface. reject him.

Outside the door of this cave red vibrates
a dream is trying to enter
it's forming in the peripheral shadows a
world I'll have always been in
for its brief duration.

I dream I dance with someone to the gooey sounds
of John Lennon's "Imagine."

Goo comes from everywhere
in and out of ass
binding blindness     Dream us
till we die

# THE STRIKE

*(October 7–December 18, 1995)*

# DANTE'S ASS A NOBLE PRIZE

*beyond love*
*another . . .*
*inclusive—*

*including the sharply bitter,*
*because that's a moral force*
*throughout universe . . .*

                      (written by left hand)
(and)

*Love can be*
*harmful, obviously,*
*as can bitterness.*

_____

You, hateful you,
may be god
That is so bitter;
go away, for now.

Physics accepts no bitterness
Creates its bomb.

_____

The subject in France is work: will there
be a shorter workweek
in twenty years' time, will one
work by contract for many
companies not one, pooled and
exactly exploited
(what subject's more important . . . )

The thing about Dante's ass . . .
the Noble Prize, or a putrified
wind through the marshes—
a rush towards a not-you a something-above-you

someone who cannot be directly addressed
except via prescribed utterances, offerings
(we're so *afraid of* great you, you Noblist)

This is bitter, though, un-
positively tangy—
I despise it, and it isn't
a fertile
death.

I wouldn't want to be pooled
as a poet Or would I?
Seamus Heaney and I exploited together i.e.
treated as equals

Might be interesting, a sort of sharing
of publication opportunities.

Accept deregulation,
the only correct economic color.
There are people in charge who know this
they know what they know
they are somewhat starlike, visible
perhaps a rare kind of sewage rat
high up where History leaks its shit which
these rats feed on first

I soul, dark doll, write so.
I will no longer be defined by the few any few.
And there are worlds awaiting exact definition
by a woman for the first time—
there is a universe only observed, considered, measured, worshipped

through men, male eyes. But you have
never been my I

Hi, says Mitch-ham, Hiya Fuckface!
I laugh.

---

The black virgin of Chartres a bed doll—

not like that—

I mean

you still can't see me at all, as change.

---

Thankfully the mineral-and-air
bitter universe
wins, over men.

Those caves beneath Alps
And go in.

Look look at that light

I want to be dark
blacker than you.
Shine on me you won't show me through
won't be
bad light in my head.

---

Write more blindly blackly
without
without anything

# PARTICLE DOLL

any child has millions of minutes of difference lavished upon it.

There is a mask of difference on your face
above your (my) naked body

under that mask, there's another, mask of sameness.
But under that . . .

_____

Stories of cave and prehistory by a darkdoll:
(dollmouth moves:)

"and I told you we were heirlooms already.
waiting . . .
not much more to add, ever, in history.
The human closes itself off
serves square container of self emotions,
often in group—
you tell I it's okay
to be a jerk, I likes the way it feels
so is a jerk."

What "you" do I look for if I am so happy alone?
god is a kiss-pants, ass-heart, is that all?

_____

Hardwood says, I'm bolstering you,
the others need you, your darkdoll "money"

That's easy, easy to give, I say.
Much harder to give away
my ordinary money.

There's a huge national strike, in France, today
Can I move at all?
'Cause government employees didn't get a raise
Will we get mail
I don't think so . . . will have to
give myself mail, transport.
Not to mention a raise.

What do I look like? keep seeing the face of
brownskinned porcelain doll with long hair—
in the mirror I'm fifty, "white" but brownish, hair greying
chopped off below ears.

Darkdoll's thick lashes made out of real hair.
Her eyes are amber clear.
Rosebud mouth, because she's a doll
Talking, as I write it down, down in the caves:
". . . universe *is* hope, except for this nothing planet, and
flows outward from my face, for instance."

I'm her face now:

and flowing out from this forest

write myself a letter:

You dreamed you were delighted to be betrayed.
Personal betrayal is found to be
gratifying, by all concerned.
You always knew this capacity for bad behavior
existed in others. Now it's true, and in your horror you're gleeful
you can begin to wage war of sorts
whichever sort of war suits your ethics
(have the reaches
of the universe heard of your ethics?)

The bitterest part of being a doll
is how to tell you
I hate how you make me this doll—
sitting propped up at dinner party or poetry panel.

"You're such a hostile doll."

You don't know my attributes
I hate you.

Now I have no attributes
back in the forest, none, black
primarily a target for loose dreams.
Random stories
possess me an instant each:
Is it true that there are no stories
elsewhere in the universe
and unconsciousness elsewhere contains no dreams?

I am composed of particles which are
different from me—
though you categorize me as Particle Doll.
If you fuck with my brain change my particles, chemicals
you'll perceive a different me
as far as you're
concerned, but you've never
really perceived *me* anyway.

I dream I'm in Rapallo though it's Collobrières
two contemporary poets are constructing
a huge eye: they climb up on the scaffolding
with an enormous cannon shape
it's mascara—they brush it on

The new eye is both cosmeticized and sexed.

I don't want to be cradled, comforted, beloved.

One thing I like about you is your weirdness
no matter how you cover it
your human parts are weird on you
your ears and nose, your breasts and prick
are ungainly
you're a Martian, a hatrack
your tits are goiters and your cunt is outlandish
Penthouse thinks you're really cute
with your slingshot bra hanging off your right goiter
the look of sexual power on your face
is absolutely stupid.

Can I now begin to see myself

A real dark face above my white nakedness?

From before
evolution I find
us, despite it

# THERE ISN'T MUCH TO DO IF YOU AREN'T GEOLOGY

watching fish in scallop-bottomed shoal
I'm in a vision.
There's a faint far mountain, The Mountain,
inside which the dead live.
I'm alone no you.
I catch a fish in a basket, what shall I
do with it eat it raw—am I so dependent? . . .
If I don't eat    And if I don't eat . . .
How do I know I must eat? Who are the dead?

There aren't the dead yet, there are only
the rulers of the Underworld
waiting for me the First Woman so
that they will have a subject.

———————————————

I read last week in a magazine
we're all descended from a common
ancestor—who apparently didn't fuck
a second common ancestor to generate us.

———————————————

How did I get here
but this is a dream
in a dream you simply know you belong
have always been in this plot:

      e.g. I'm in Needles with two friends who
      are disgusted at the new law
      that all cactuses must be turned off
      by 7 a.m. each morning—so they won't bloom.
      Another friend has gone out to turn off all our cactuses.
      We watch through a window as,
      at the row of parked cactuses, he turns the bud on each,

its knob-like protruberance, so that the cactus
can't bloom all day: it would be red.

———————————————

Back at the vast primal lake
I've generated Hardwood without thinking
or did I think him?
No one ever "thought me"
how did I get here I didn't "get here"
He doesn't say anything today
The authors of this myth say there's no speech yet.

———————————————

The water itself
was turbulent first, a massive
body full of seeming shapes which
might be called anything
gods, forces, equations, any word or projection.

———————————————

Lewd dance, a flamenco for a couple:
she's suddenly on all fours skirt up,
he's arousing her with his hand;
they're fully clad and she's even wearing
long 19th century drawers.
See the outline of vaginal lips
through white cotton.

———————————————

We will bind our left hands with our right—
water with water.

I stand naked
on the smallest sandbar there might be,

you whom I love, receding or encroaching
salt. Sit down and think, that is,
observe the light and shape not quite geometric
in the fluid other.

———————————————

E-mail, Internet
there are so many ways to learn more
keep in touch
as if the chaotic waters of you
weren't near enough.

---

Is I or you a demented
baglady
I mean is god that, pulling
universe
out of
random bags.

You have foolishly seen fit to
call it harmonious, or delicately
chaotic
as it suits you, this universe, as you see it
in Your Job.

---

I gave in and worried about "my abilities"
all
afternoon . . .

But aside from that, you physicists,
what do you think of
sexual flamenco?
Was it once water, water
and now it's the art of
degradation, beautifully performed?
Why not someone might say. Why not degradation?

When it returns
to water, who will see it in the waves
clitoris and the hand
touching
it which is
your blind eye

the physicist's blind
eye

# AND STILL NO STORY, HOW WILL YOU KNOW WHEN IT'S OVER?


into dark cave     Who is here
another man
telling a story
do I have to listen?

"While consciousness came to us stealthily . . . "
something like that.

"The universe *is* consciousness," I scream at him,
"that's all there is!"
Calm down, says everyone.

"And part of consciousness is unconsciousness,"
I continue. "Or vice versa. What's the difference?
Some buzz of memory?
gas in your car for one and not the other?
You *pay* in consciousness, so it's primary, precious,
it's so *financed* . . .

but down here our memory's different,
death memory, rock memory, water memory
all one being me too. Being mind."

_____


Went to London and performed
in the Royal Albert Hall
with 15 others . . .

scream for attention and get it
Why?
Dream that the hall has crumbled, is overgrown

with brambly roses. Stars and moon through
the broken ceiling. We're dead, conscious, or
the way one's technically unconscious
while conscious in a dream . . . Skip that, I mean
we can't have fun here anymore. Go

But that's not a dream that's the future.

———————————————

. . . This is a shape, a prow of a boat
the ship of death is lit up on deck

aglow and I get to
get to

but I can't remember.

———————————————

Stop giving time so much gas, Hardwood says
Right.

Time is another manly construction
a name for the wrinkles
on a woman's face?
a name for all our conventions

Caught caught caught in it
tripped up
I'll give my life to your time

The worst of your conventions is
that I'm you, part of us.

———————————————

Falling asleep in the afternoon
I keep seeing dreams start . . .
There's a dream
Whole story's contained in a cell
if I brush its edge frontally

the story's there all at once, I don't have to
"go through it"

if it comes to me when I'm not looking
I experience the story
chronologically.

---

29 people were injured by Tuesday's bomb,
four seriously,
who suffered amputations.

---

I dream that
a bomb might injure me
because some Muslims hate me. I mean
isn't that real possibility a dream,
wouldn't its happening be dreamlike?

 . . . if hatred's a vicious phantasm,
waking reality's a dream.

So do we hate you, dreaming . . .

I hated that woman, in last night's dream,
loved for the dresses men love in this culture,
as you love the dresses you've
designed for your women.

I don't want to hate
To find fault's so dreamlike.

Why don't we make some new emotions?

---

Did dreams begin when women were first
excluded from public life?

Drink up, Hardwood says.
Just because men own time
doesn't mean you can't have a good one.

Oh sure, a virtual drink.

———————————————

I know you despite time and inside its caves.
Between minutes, is where I know you
the time between minutes grows into a dream
a roseate space—like one of these poems
always here, and nowhere at no time

# MORE OF THE ASSHOLES OF GIANTS

into the rock room where
people sit listening to what poet . . .
black suit, oiled lock of hair, black
string tie: "I am Ordure the techno preacher . . .
On Line. Let *me* define your future"
(Let me, let me, cry voices from other wires.)

I'm older this week, is that the future,
would like to suffer loss of definition—
though not of exactitude—
please for my fiftieth birthday.

---

If the real rulers of the world
are not only not elected
but unrecognized as such
will they have as much fun?
Bill Gates' picture again, an unsatisfied mind,
on the leaves falling
from the techno trees in your heart.

---

The door once might have
slammed shut     on anyone
because she wasn't like     Rich & Boland
names on the door of the Poetry Firm.
But they are not future Gates
they are as obsolete now as
old money badly invested.

Yet a poem still works
This is how a poem works

uses us, uses you to make itself

These are the real
Windows     still
in the lines between my sections.

---

Stride out onto the beach—
local artists at work there.
"I'm painting with yellow," one says, "blue and yellow.
Sky's always yellow in a storm
and there's always a storm these days.
Now watch, this is how I make my telephone poles":
In a quasi-Japanese calligraphic style.

---

In international heart there's no dearth of particulars
fuck the sacrosanct local, this is everyone's storm.
I'm old enough for a disrespect undreamed of,
because now the exactly
insouciant soul's speaking again:
you wanted me, you got me. Exactly as I am. I'm no convention.

---

". . . if we're to remain players in the States and Germany . . ."
is the kind of thing men say around me on my fiftieth birthday.

---

In Paris polluted like Mexico City
say the word 'diary' disparagingly?
(as in, is this just a *diary*?)

Chirac had a cross of Lorraine laid out
like an airfield last night at Invalides, red and
marked by candleflames, and cops,
a pageant in honor of lingering death:
DeGaulle's, a frightening worship.

If this is a diary
is it worthless
like life?

Climbing down into asshole of that adored one
see written the words "fecal heart"—
well shit on my dearest
country what grows your crops, eh?
If it doesn't smother you, his largesse.

Come out of there, the next, and the next:
days, contrived by our father.
And if you make it, in whatever country, in
whatever way it's the same Good Brown. As I say
over and over, exposing our "Heart."

Now your particles, shit *particles*
formerly swept away
by Tiamat bitter soul water
are they no longer water soluble?
Or maybe, soul refuses to absorb them any longer.

Must darken, must walk off
to the left, and climb down
Follow the usual narrow stream
through caverns . . .
my face is very dark today.

There is a golden city way under here
I didn't know that. Approach it, glints
of gold electricity in pastel air

We are all dark but the city is light.
I don't understand what this means.
Hardwood I mean Mitch-ham
must detect again.

"Fair city exists
when you're dark enough
that's all," he says.

He drops cigarette grinds it with heel
into fair street,
"I had to do that just once."
"Where are the authorities of this city?"
"Just you, and your You," he replies.

———————————————

My father is around. young smiling . . .
white porcelain cups . . . we drink light.
When you're dead and wrapped up in your experience
you won't have to be good—the soul isn't
good, it's more.

What would I do here, in this bright
bookcover land

# RITA, A RED ROSE, HATES HER CLOTHES

where I am's a roomful of clothes
finding the right ones to wear.
I don't want to give my concert naked.
Or do I. How naked am I now,
as a poem?

---

"Naked"
          consists of a flesh-colored garment.
Like the flesh-colored bathing suits movie actresses
wore for nude scenes in the 50's.

"Clothes" consists of dress designs,
fake necklines and outlines
delineated on a flesh-colored garment

Who's ever been naked?

---

There's too much light in this cavern—
I think it's behind a large eye
What happens if I
walk out through the eye?

---

Flesh-colored suit with
mathematical equations encircling it

A matching skullcap a map of the brain and
          its functions:
scientific fashions.

But I know *my* equations are right!
if I were a particle scientist you'd give me a prize.

Light from the boring "real world" threatens
to soak through the cave eye corrupting my darkness
I back away
I'm naked
and dark.

---

In the métro, I prefer to the singers
a songless beaten-down man
who haunts the Louis Blanc line
asking people in the métro cars, one by one,
for *"une pièce."*

---

This is not the Whitman Intersection.

I see quietly

not walking out through the eye
into the blazing light of the Mystics
mingling with all

I    am    absolutely    not    You.

---

Oh no now I'm dressed as Rita the rose
with redpetal cloth bunched up over my breasts
and also down from the waist
leaving my legs bare
the skirt though is
long in the back, I look like Geena Davis
on Academy Awards night
the year of that female buddy movie
which contained no witticisms.

I'm wearing the Rose Dress
to a concert
Howlin' Wolf at the Hungry i
I'm going to let another man sing at me . . .

unless I myself can be
Howlin' Wolf. Or is it Whitman.

Hey,
can I be welcomed to
the Grand Intersection of You
and sing at the Hungry i?
Not as a humble *citoyenne*, speck
in the poet's vast I,
but as    the famous I    itself?
A Multitude of Men rush to assure me
you can only approach the cosmic I in all humility.
Like us, they say, so Fucking Back Off.

———————————————

I am absolutely not you
not even you girls.
No witless movie, genre or mystical.
Fuck off Walt, all of you.

———————————————

. . . surrounded by shed snakeskins,
including a small albino one, and a large one with
poison sacs.

That was one dream. Now

sitting in the sun alone
jeans and an old red shirt
The Turtle Mountains, The Old Woman Mountains,
Iron Mountain, The Spirit Mountains
all out there . . .
fantasy, since I'm in Paris,
but do somehow sit on a rock in the desert
and wonder where the snakes are—
tiniest breeze
in a desert holly bush.

———————————————

Let's go back into caves
and talk to my willpower Hardwood
he's laughing at a snakejoke
"when is a snake naked
when it's a nake with no S
snake with no hiss . . ."

Would I want to be a nake, Hardwood?
does Alice Notley want to be a nake

# AN IMPECCABLE SEXISM I MEAN AN ELEGANT IDEA OR PROCEDURE HAUNTS THE STARS

there is something that exists that I can't think of can't imagine

_____

Where did the first matter come from
a thought or extrusion from
elsewhere, but

what
shit it free . . .

There's infinity in my imagination,
but I can't imagine the infinite.

_____

'Think that unthinkable thought!'
'Get away from me, you Holy Man!'

'The Laws of the Universe must be Elegant.'
Push a baby out of your snatch then see if you believe that.

_____

At the beginning
is all this consciousness
already there, screaming in pain
at the intensity of the heat, the explosion?

A sweet young thing
gave birth on the beach on _Baywatch,_ last night,
gasping in French in pain in Malibu, California.

_____

Hardwood's trenchcoat is flapping a lot today.
He looks decrepit, dewlapped, squinty-eyed, perhaps from morning beers
we sit down in a dark cave so he can widen his eyes.

'A messy a bloody flux
becomes "symmetry":
the supposed miracle of
eight leaves on a stem
just for You and your brain contemplating them . . .'

'Let's not have sarcasm today,' Hardwood says, 'I'm hungover.'

I must go further down into the caves alone then.

———————————————————

Walking further downstairs shrouded in black crepe head to toe
Why? Because I'm insignificant and must die?

You, you are all as insignificant
as a woman, dead in childbirth
in another century. In the universe which
you investigate, you have no status.
Your equations, and my writings
are dissolved gone dust. So

Walking walking down
and down
            Below the grave

help me, Who, You? to have
a new "feeling" . . .

I still look mourning, Spanish
my darkness today is heavy clothes.

Now I seem to be Irene Papas, the Greek actress.

———————————————————

I've come out by the sea my skirt's beginning to float in the water
there is no freedom.
Bill Gates is free, but he's a jerk.
A jerk jerks off
and the semen floats away
and now the shore's lined with men jerking off

and their semen floats away and then they panic
they jump into the water and swim after it.
It disappears, they have to jerk off some more.

———————————————

That's the sort of thing
the imagination really "does."

On another planet, or dead,
one might be "free."

Life doesn't have to be human
I can be dead and inhuman, molecules floating.

———————————————

The sea is polluted with your efforts
the tide is rising against my black dress—but
what's the difference etcetera.
The difference is there might have been life.

———————————————

Let's have a page of Good Writing here.

(Lack of interest.)

———————————————

I creep back into the cave
and go lie down in my grave
I have been buried in wet black crepe
edged with sparkling semen.

———————————————

You could work out a set of equations
involving technology and stupidity
something like Hardwood's Constant,
the exact figure for the increase in stupidity
in proportion to the advance in technology; or maybe
j=ts squared or to whatever power,
a figure for the general jacking off the two produce together.

Is it all just jacking off? Hardwood screams into my grave
Get up and fight, he shouts. No, I say sitting up,
there's some oral sex involved . . .

Our Civ: a photo which when viewed upsidedown—
the way we've usually viewed it—depicts flesh
abstractly, lovely. Rightsideup it's obviously
just a woman giving a rock star a blowjob.

---

I can't get out of this poem
it's Your poem
you're making me make it this way
it's us, this poem is alive
even if it's ugly or I'm dead
it's the City of You even if you aren't "in it"

# BREAKING THE SOUND BARRIER

there is    a river
called the River    of No    Return . . .
Young Mitch-ham, you starred in that movie.
What a stained color of life that was then—
bright northern blue and green.

---

In the new consciousness
I'm being shown a browner hand
            against
the denuded trees
near Invalides Métro, last night.

---

Sky dark sky
begins to eclipse a cabbage rose . . .

I committed some sort of dull treason
last night, in my dreams,
simply by flying out of
the golden-bronze map of New York.
The newspapers said that
those who'd caught airplanes
from *there,* as I had, *were*
guilty of treason.

---

I'm very happy to leave the Us
in my lack of plurality
with my weak left-handedness
to guide me to nowhere at all.

I'm breaking the sound barrier.
Faster than explanation, know it first. hear it see it

The Bad Hand Mountain looms.

Mitch and I climb it on donkeys.

I meet my mother there,
Sit down, she says.

A man comes out dancing slowly. He is The Mountain
I mean   he is   the mountain.

I dance, giving off light.
All of the shelves inside me are empty.
The Mountain says, Treason is a great freedom.

A line is attacking attaining.
It's my snake.
My mother puts my snake around my shoulders
it hisses like crazy.

Back on the other side of the barrier
the tap is leaking rhythmically in the kitchen—
I'm really enjoying it—
two sounds, a tap and a splash sometimes
tap   tap   tapsplash.

In the sound booth
there isn't much
on this disc of the moon
on this disc in the center there isn't much to do.

I'm sleeping right now aren't I Mitchell
Arise and stand up to the shits, stand at their table, he says,

A raft going through the rapids
of the River of No Return.

---

I am no longer damaged.

I went to the white elevator.

Let the Koh-i-noor in . . .

I am integral diamond.

---

The people don't mind
they have to break their doors
pull them, Silence, along:

The people are fucked up.

---

I'm thinking in a new . . .

there are the conquering fires
piss on them from our height.

This place I think from, behind words
is from before fixed doors.

Sell it to you?
A man wants me to sell the idea of this poem to him . . .
Sell it! Sell it! voices shout
like shouting "Take it off!" at a strip show.

---

Have wroth
primary ribs—

That means you've pissed off Adam
says Hardon.

no return no return

There was never any similarity
between myself and prices.

_____

 . . . Winternet, the sadness of River
of No Return
technological river . . .

oh, technologically, I want to go back
would go backwards
if I could

# THE MORBID MANAGERS ARE SERVING TRAYS OF CHARNEL FLESH

flat flowers blooming everywhere
predicted by Andy Warhol—
they're nasty and flat.

---

Future females
are not the same as
future people,
no such prediction.
And I haven't been predicted, have I.
"Your face keeps
bleeding outside the flower's outline," Hardwood says.

---

There are some poets who are surely
technicians, modern technicians
they really love to discuss (endorse) their product
like on the Cyberscope page of *Newsweek*
I don't want to be part
everyone's idiots. have I said this before
two thousand five hundred trillion times . . .

We're on strike again today in France
we're living in a political past
that probably hasn't ever quite existed.
It's vaguely familiar though, the way
some imagined American past
flickers through the "works" of Dole and Gingrich
or as in poetry a policied reality flickers
across the face of Your poem text experiment.

In this story-dream, Mitch and I
bought a kit from the captain of our ship
obviously a Reality Captain—
it consisted of the heads of dead monkeys
with slots in them where "cards" could be inserted
for the all-important "game":
Just like Your job? To guess the cards in Your
opponent's dead-monkey's head?

In Part Two of this dream
a young brown boy—who was he?—was tricked by elders—
was I one? or was I he?—into entering the territory of lepers
skull-ghouls who lived in their own tombs—
because then he could never leave it, would be their necessary servant.

It happens when you're about four.

I know this is true.

I am SO outmoded, as a mind is.
I don't even know if I WANT to be used by
the future . . .

I enter the cave of my company Real Mind
and it is nowhere in this world

flat flat flat the sound once more of
my feet on rock, and Tiamat
leading me downward into selfdom
"pure and simple." All it ever.
Who's here today? Some lepers actually.
Is this a City of You?

Speak to me ghoul

'Mind breathes
better air,' it says.

Have there been more messages?
'Keep in touch with your fears—
respect your ghouls,' it says.

'. . . preschool teacher will be here'
'. . . that's what I think, those schools are, you know,
ready for Helen Vendler . . .'

The other lepers are chatting.

———————————————

And so one leper says, we're your sick fears
aging and death, sure but a stale life decaying
in other people's world, an exact imagination
that bears increasingly little resemblance to your own.

The leper pauses,

And yet you say you're no longer damaged . . .
But *we're* still down here.

You're . . . friends, I say, if you're my fears, though in the dream
you were hell and
there was no happiness.

———————————————

There was another, slippery, territory
a floor where my feet slid in muck
a miserable room
where a man named Mark shit bloody shit
into a small chamberpot.

———————————————

What is anyone marked for
use of our apples, I told you.

The pain of this French strike's considerable
being against intricacies of policy
not being against
life for example as we know it.

If a little boy or man is Mark and I am Markette myself,
a commercial territory    let me offer you peaches
my sins, this is another one—in a good world
I might not feel like writing poems
would I be happy

# THE BIG SLIP ON THE DEAD WOMAN IS PINK

people tired on feet or trapped in cars
at polluted sunset;
empty three-quarter moon over Louvre
will hang over States later.

———————————————

Mitch-ham is huge today, but
"What can I do in this strike?"
Pushes his hat
back. Sits
down.

It will happen
a man will sit there
brave and fair.

. . . I meant to make a mouth for
a finer place like the far sky,
that will not hurt us, as we hurt ourselves?

No, I'm enjoying making mean remarks about everyone,
because I am the Soul, misunderstood
I'm pure, wise, and bitchy: that's not
contradictory. I intend to be grouchy throughout my eternity.

———————————————

People keep trying to foist Greats on me—oh
Wordsworth Melville Langston Hughes, James Joyce, or
some girl, Bradstreet Dickinson, Stein Toni Morrison
        Fuck 'em—
They aren't "great" on the newly discovered
planet beneath Orion; and deep deep inside me, in the caverns
I haven't heard of them. I've only heard of the unnamed there

What will France   do   will it change
my story? No métro bus or train, no
mail possible cuts in
electricity for some, the students on strike.

---

Hugh I mean Huge Hardwood, what are you up to

What's happened is that the Soul
is trying to detect the detective, Will
Why   To make something "happen."

---

The bead of bitterness is leading us Mitch through a tunnel
Veers to left . . . a hoary meadow, middle of pines . . . I'm
freezing: I once saw double here, he says,

I saw Cold and Warm at the same time.
They cancelled each other out, producing a void where
anyone might put a song.

(Song)

The unwinding sky
wants to be what
we haven't named.

This could be called Consciousness
Though it may be silly, Consciousness:
What comes of it is.

---

Why are you larger, Hardwill?
So I can help you get this right.

---

I look at Will he's a gold man a foil man
with a gold maskface and no clothes but gold
a material skin with wavy dark lines on it

It isn't silly enough, he says, it's too beautiful:
That's why I look like a detective instead.

Silly enough for what?
This life.

---

Now we're back in a cave, where a message has been left:
"THE SLIP IS HARD IF NOT BIG."

I can't understand it    Clothing?
Transgression, Mitch says, The Big Slip, the terrible remake I starred in.
That was almost twenty years ago.
The world now is more Remake plus new Techno
empty, dangerous.

---

I'm trying to be as clear as possible
as unfictional as possible, given that I have allowed
"fiction" in.
What I make is marked by fiction
Am I mostly our collective one, that I keep
trying to change, at least for myself?
No. Not now.

---

Speaking outside the fiction: I dreamed the foil man,
sexless beautiful and gold, and I knew he was Will when I awoke.

---

And there was a gold, or "pet" cat in another dream
who was surely dangerous, with the facial structure
the large-boned head and wide jaw of a lion or panther
"*Il est dangereux, oui, mais il est beau,*" said his owner.
He may be my will too

## DANCING INTO THE SHADOWS OF THE HIDEOUS FUTURE CITY WE DON'T THINK SO DURING THIS STRIKE

one reason the story
is discontinuous is that it is,

as each day I wake up neutral
outside of any story, for awhile

That is so great.

———————————————

Huddled against cave wall
dressed in a sketchy-skirted tutu, pink
am little girl from ad I saw outside
Galeries Lafayette on Monday? or
am girl version of transvestite ballerina,
dressed in red, I dreamed of last night.
Sometimes I was her, sometimes
I was painting her. "I like those shadows," she said
of my painting. "They aren't shadows," I said.
They weren't. They were just paint.

———————————————

I was very beautiful but at a certain
point it dawned on me that
I had a penis to hide.

I had a prick but my lover didn't know
        I
don't know it, myself, except intellectually

In this dance there are no
real organs. No joke

there's no joke without pricks and cunts.

———————————

Staring into unsexed death very black no joke.

———————————

The sex organ under Your tutu,
god or You—

some sort of evolutionary flourish
as species-specific as chiaroscuro is culture-specific?

"I" "believe" "that."

Today
I will walk
to Galeries Lafayette, to go shopping.
That's about as interesting as linguistic philosophy.

———————————

Alain Juppé, *le premier ministre*
presented himself to the public last night on TV
for the first time since the strikes began . . .

deft, "reasonable," telling his story

All American tellings seem dramatic and coarse
compared to French ones

That's why, Mitch-ham
that's why I am a ham pink as a tutu,
and in extremes blood red.

A snowflake kept falling behind Juppé,
through the window,
like the same snowflake.

———————————

I've never wanted a lumpy crotch
a more of penis ugh. Juppé's or anyone's

politely intrudes, doesn't it, mine's here now
my prick or my cunt
I am a soul I have both and none
I don't think it's snowing this morning—
do You read *Newsweek* it never knows one thing

You   are   *Newsweek*.

---

And there are shadows ahead
            shadows ahead
            shadows ahead
      of the city.
                    (Repeat)

---

Suddenly in the loving caves without preliminary
and press self to the cool stone wall, which is more affectionate
than You are, unless it *is* You.
As I blame You and blame You.

---

What does the wall say
"Problematic when
hearts are red and greens twine—
who sees a love spell everywhere
sees wrongly sees
a story set in place by some past.
Who sees love sees
only a story."

---

Walk down one level then
Golden City's there today but it's a stage play not
a reality, audience of dark heads watching
I can hardly see—

the ballet dancer comes onstage in red, kicks up leg
there's the outline of her penis
it's small and under the crotch, not frontal.

I suppose she's me: now are You still in love with me?

_____

Do You love me, You profess to:
I'm disgusted by the idea
of being loved by the cosmic other or by society

or by professional lovers of others: poets, prophets, politicians.

I do want to be loved
for my genitals, which make me anyone.

_____

Mitch-ham says, Do you have the balls
to continue this poem?

This poem is a home for my mind

I must be genie-flecked, or genuflect

# WHITE RICE WORDS ARE THE MEANS OF EXCHANGE

there are many green hills in the duvet

Call the caves up to street level

see if I can call "sub" or "un" up into the quotidian.

―――――――――――――――――

What's the name of the students who overturn cars
in the demonstrations . . . *casseurs*

Want more money for education
so they can have futures
with money in them. Money has won.

These are
pervasively conservative
times.

―――――――――――――――――

I dreamed, let's see, that in order to explain
to someone the tenets of a certain sect of poets
I had to buy a packet of rice.
The rice, like a book, explained their beliefs.
But, I had no money;
he, though poor, happened to have
four dollars and twenty-five cents, the price of
       this rice including tax,
"and nothing better to spend it on."

Rice? why rice—

the works of this (real) sect
are bland and white and numerous
though this was basmati rice
a more expensive form of colorless nutrition

Rice swells: oh do they.

---

On Front Street Upfront Street, with its sidewalk tables
near the railroad station, I always get caught in
hard struggles. Between those tables and a store
further down the street. I'm trying to resolve . . .
the money maybe, that I have none for my "old age."
No mail, on Front Street today; no money if you don't *earn* it,
make a go of swelling something sticky and white.

---

What have I earned.

earned is E is thee.

They've opened a métro station for
the homeless to go in, during the strike.
The homeless are not
anyone's thee. I am not a thee in France . . .
as I am not a thee to
several poetry sects; or to Newt Gingrich
(will that name survive much longer? should
I keep naming him?)

---

These are such conservative times
(repeat)

Instead of descending into the caves today I again
climb out of them, with long subconscious dark hair
I bring another dream with me
of living on the street and travelling in a group including infants
jungle cats will attack them if we camp here
on this urban sidewalk tonight, there is a
leopard dark with light spots small but dangerous
can we afford a cheap hotel, we find a single bunk somewhere.

The surface of my (real) life will never be secure.

I've dragged the caves up with me

This is the message on the wall:

"Your words are all as material
as pennies. more fucking pennies

In conservative times beware of the word Communication."

I pull the caves lightly
around me
shawl-like.

Mitch, you're heavy lidded.

We're united, he says, I'm asleep.

I the Soul Alice am congested from pollution
walking in the cars as numerous as words online—
I think I don't care if I die. except
What if there's a human afterlife?

These are all the things I don't say to people
to their faces. I, like any poor bastardess
intimidated by anyone's air of Authority.
But who would I care to speak to anyway?
Wake up Mitch and soften me—I usually harden
you, he says—Soften me, I say.

Thee, who are thee

(such an unmagical view of life we have
unimaginative, material as words)

# SEEMS TO BE HEADING FOR MEXICO

my dark soulcore splits off from me
wandering red rock canyons
where people on horseback are tiny
and spotted like blackbirds.

———————————————

Spent all my dreamtime last night washing dishes
while the Glasgow poet babbled to me.
This morning I read about the 'privileging
by hegemonic positivistic anthropologists
of ocular metaphors for knowledge, refusing to accept
the evidence of historical "silences.' "

———————————————

Soulcore's silence screams at the author
she is much of me, Alice, in no
way that You have systematized

A god or "Holy Person"    if you should see her    as I do

She's wearing a black crepe veil
the length of her face.

———————————————

Hardwood and I will find her again
having left our horses behind we wind through rock walls.
I'm rather empty he's quiet it's Sunday morning
December in France of the outer world.

In these stories of myself I,
there she is ahead now walking across a more desert expanse.

It seems to be night now in mind
fox licks her face she's asleep in the hills . . .

A joke for this sitch, Mitch? Why is she heading for
the border?—Others have bored her, he says.
Truthfully though, mysterious rites
entertain a soul

Poetry's less fun now.
They say we used to be amused,
and that was why we were. Why we existed
Who's amused now?

Mitch and I are getting very sunburned.
We wear dark Mexicanish clothes, studded with conchos.
We just can't keep up with her, but

Suddenly I am her a moment:

'going to the country of sleep.
Not to waken to disrespect for my practice . . .

> *shitty stars I know 'em*
> *I know what they are.'*

Her footsteps very determined and quick—
we've walked a lot during the strike—
and found it difficult to keep amused—
you could lose your soul to ranting.

"I think we'd better perform a rite," Hardwood says.

Hardwood the Artifact
leftover from such ancient usage
as Will and Soul and Rite
conducts the rite.

We sit down together on a boulder.
He chants softly:

> When the soul leaves the house like a lace bird, black,
> call it back—call it back—
> black black as your self, it comes back.
>
> When    the soul of your soul leaves
> call it back with black candy
> entice it with licorice sweets    til it's back.

He sprinkles black sand in a circle around us.

---

Words whirl
select what I want

Soulcore's come back, remarkably darker
of skin and dress
near faceless
I see her in mind this morning at nine, I'm

shaken by her reality (in my mind) her opacity

Stay as opaque as you are.

---

I am primal, primary, and so *am* opaque.

Stay, but I wasn't changing or leaving. I
had gone off to think. In a sulk, of course

Conclusion: I just am

I am more primary than particles. self-evident—
Soulcore says

# BEING WITH PEOPLE A CLICHE   EATING   DINNER

"I love my Pocahontas but not my Us."

_____

I don't know what city
sometimes it's a loft
sometimes it's a street, blocked off to cars
I have some loves I only love, sons
I rush towards them at the end of that street
later in the loft I see the older set I am part of
I shall not forgive us . . . forgiveness in this way,
compassion, an evil—a self-indulgence—a civ
which fetishizes personal exigencies
above those in the sick air we bequeath to others.

_____

The Pocahontas Doll the Little Whore.

_____

There should be a Slut Doll this Xmas
tarty short dress and blatant stocking tops
some bullshit in her hair, some glitterbit jewelry there—
Her name   is   Ewe   or   OO.

_____

Stoop down in evening street
and gather up in arms a small
domain, lit, the canyon which
I descend daily. I just picked it up in my arms—
wearing a cloth coat like a 50's woman's.
It seemed to happen outside the newsstand
on rue du Faubourg-Poissonnière around the corner.

In the caves several bodies cluster together
like elementary particles.
They pull away from the center
their nucleus is the Slut Doll, live, I've described.
She's wearing a tatty fur stole and has a
silly hat on her head. Her name is Miss Bangles the
Princess Jo-Mama.
Saucery eyes and so friendly.

Now, proceeding to the right:
There's the Compassion Room . . .
Who's in it waiting for Compassion? A suited man
and a workshirted man, Business, and Labor,
in the blue-smoke air in there she will give them
some Compassion.

If I have to go outside again today
into the air of the twentieth day of the strike:
cars like roaches in a darkened tenement kitchen
under the sink—
I mean I do have to go outside and will come back
with pollution-caused pusbags under my eyes.

The shirts in power, poetry power,
still want a decorous poetry.

Another possibility, always, is "linguistic fireworks."

Falling asleep with emeralds and pearls swirling in front of me
the windows on the rue de la Paix I walk past . . .

Alexander Reza has placed fish tanks in its windows
and dunked, dangled, ruby-and-diamond necklaces among the little fishies.

Compete Compete COMPETE! the world screams at France—
this gross wickedness assented to by everyone,
including the puniest Anglo-American journalist . . .

What a nice person! X says of a perfect scumbag
I mean, who isn't. a nice person.

---

Slut Doll, besides being "Compassion,"
a stiff clit and the question of who strokes it,
is also Psychology, that wornout ancient game.
I've dreamed about her before, in a red dress at a sock hop:
"I'm unable to grieve for Burgess!" she said to me melodramatically
I hovered between caring and not caring, then chose not caring.

---

No, Hardwill, I don't know if there's
a way out of this thought.
It leads further and further in—
this negativity is the truth the way out is out the
other side who knows where but no where anyone's ever
been. Optimism is irrelevant. The journey through
bitter thought, is important.
I, Soul, am certainly not important:
and really have nothing "personal" to lose.

Mitch's hat casts a shadow on his vast face
as the will darkens to work.
I'm watching him he's no longer just The Actor
he's more mysterious, less acculturated
though still capable of camping it up.

---

"I love my friends    and relatives too
I'll forsake them all    and go with you"

That was the Queen of Hearts to the Ace of Sorrow,
or perhaps in this poem, vice-versa, or both.
Very pretty

# IN THE MOTHERLESS, HOMOGENIZED
# AND E-EPISTOLARY

the Black Queen and the White King
meet on their chessboard
in a French coffee ad, for *Carte Noire,*
*un café nommé désir.* They dance
in the swirling darkness
created by erotic coffee. They remember.
Popinjay terrestrials remember.

The strike may be ending after today's big *manif.*
Marc Blondel, of the occasionally-CIA-funded FO, quoted in Trib
to the effect that this govt. must realize
the French don't want to live like motherfucking Anglo-Saxons.

Down deep, rockward
and I take the heart hat off my head
my popinjay heart off my popinjay head.

———————————————

Preview of collapse
of the non-Anglo-Saxon world of France and others,
which must later fall to an Asian world of even harder labor?
Who would have thought it would be so difficult to live?
easy as breathing, as walking and sleeping
as popping a grub into your mouth.

And I even have a "talent," poetry.
I'm not really supposed to use it
not if it interferes with my ability
to pay for my dotage, to pay for the *cheminots'*
right to continue to retire at fifty, which
they have struck long and hard for.

. . . a midnight-blue shawl for my fiftieth,
from Mexico.

---

The drinks are too strong for these children,
a group of them. The very young
Keshia Pullman-Knight is one, in a pink tutu.
They're drinking things like Slivovitz and Cointreau:
no one can even finish one, no one but me

in a military compound that's probably a nuclear plant—
that looks like one of those monoliths along the Loire.
Sabrina of *Charlie's Angels* is a giant
has become immense trying to discover
the reactor's evil secret. Richard Basehart
the villain spy is completely alcoholic.

---

The message in the cave today
is a drawing of an eye, with the iris overlapping
its borders, slipping out
of the eye. Hardwood seems sloshed.
He smokes and stares at the eye.
He may be trying to detect the source of the messages.

---

Prozac: everyone takes it and reads prose
or less often, writes it, including most poets.
Maintaining the prose-money life You're addicted to.

---

Down by the railroad station
in more olden times in dreams
actually no one's there, Front Street is empty.

Walks solitarily onto the street
a dark unidentifiable figure
pauses, looks; a form of soul . . .
the past, the empty Harvey House
exists in her.

Can you have a face that's bigger than a nuclear plant
can you drink your hundred and fifty one proof rum
can you hold on to Basehart the vicious drunk spy
as he disappears into thin air
so you can disappear with him and find out his Secret,
so not only Men like Him will Know:
how to conduct business affairs
and international affairs, how to run a railroad?
Then you, too, my daughter, can be a man . . .

"You haven't lived till you've seen my dead and sleepless
father . . ."
said
someone.

The father's trying to remarry a young blonde
Oh Romeo she says, as a matter of fact
she is Blondel and he's power, it's
a world of lovers, but not of mothers
again. again

The world is again. again
in the hokey sadly-sadly mode.

Hardwood says to me, The messages come from you
The eye's not slipping out to merge with You, capital Y
or even small; the eye is slipping out in order
not to die, slipping out to see

# SHIT, FIRE, AND CRYSTAL

*(DECEMBER 19, 1995–MARCH 9, 1996)*

# BREAKING AN UNSOUND BARRIER . . .


between contained and uncontained eye.

But the eye has never been contained
a body
is only an approximate
location . . .

_____

I almost precisely understood my
relation to You, the other day . . .
No it wasn't to do with the fact that I was Your You
(Yours or god's) it was that
there was a hole in me that was You.
If I adjusted my periphery, which immaterially
extended like a saucer from my center,
sort of screwed it around, and I felt this in 'real life'—
I could perceive the hole, both really You and really a hole.

_____

The moth flies up with two holes painted on its wings.
Scientists say that the holes mime eyes
I say they mime you's.

So You were flooding me all day yesterday
merchants newscasters scientists celebrities
strikers government officials.

Go on down on down in the caves

where the You-hole fills with projections from my dark core
a sort of You that's I, but . . .
(help me get this right, I or You)

STOP BELIEVING, says the message,
THIS MAY BE A TEMPORARY MEASURE BUT
STOP BELIEVING.

---

I smell whisky it's Hardwood there's a non-You . . .
"You're still believing," he says.

They're going to try an extraction on me

Pull out the tooth by the roots.

A blonde pulls it out . . . "Look it's clearly bi-lingual":
it has two huge roots. "English and French?" I ask
I didn't want to lose that tooth
"Honey, it could be more like
I and you, male and female, Soul and Will,
blonde and brunette, mind and body
Western dualism of some nature"

"I DON'T NECESSARILY WANT TO LOSE THAT TOOTH!"
I'm screaming. She
puts it back in.

---

Tension.
Write something down.
Wash all the laundry piles of laundry
so it can blow away.

---

braincase    expand    shores    center    gravity    melts
quite.
hall in (haul in?)

(some interference, I hear 'zigzag' and 'quack' at the same time)

gears and monsters made out of gears
arms held up to hit: "because you're so placable!"

"I wanted a woman the come inside":
who says it, the monster?

and he child in the layer years ago . . .

(this is like LSD twenty-six years ago)

truth mop white (repeat)

live cylindrical not-you head to toe black
(pointing finger) light white grave charge


   . . .

rainbow snake over lintel of my house

     dizzy

lightning   the real atom bomb
is a hooker house.

_____

"What's all that?" asks Hardword.

"I dreamed, awake, in language . . .
dreams contain no belief

but whenever I dream in any way
the content turns to sexism

the deeper I go, that's still what I know,
is there a ground below it"

# THE VEIL IS, LIKE, SEXISM OR IS IT LIKE IT

very far down in earth, below the rooms
of previous dreams . . .
This is a small roundish chamber
a curved rectangle. I lie down to think and
the concave dirt ceiling drops nearer

But It,
the Truth, won't be a Thought.

This isn't right; I struggle up and claw at my
grave like a she-ghoul.

The truth is still trapped
somewhere in my life
between the useless actions
You make me perform.

_____

Dripping grave mold like Ms. Usher.

DON'T BELIEVE ANYTHING.

_____

I want to rend the damn veil
the holy veil spun from men's minds
because I'm pregnant and very upset.
All those guys are here to
help me do it . . . they have to get lost.

I can get pregnant anywhere anytime at
any age even when dead.

No I'm not interested in abortion rights
I want to rend that damn veil

like a big canvas roof, a tent a rough envelope
in the sky—would everyone please SHUT UP? GO
AWAY? Male and FEMALE? Or give me
great big canvas-cutting shears.

I'm wearing a white shroud
with famous thinkers in pixyl dots all over it
I HATE IT! Would you tell the goddamned folksingers and
rappers to shut up PLEASE!!

---

Diehard Parisians line up for their Xmas chocolates,
their foie gras, muscat, champagne.
A woman with an unpleasant voice demands
pretty boxes for everything. Is this an allegory
of the strike?
         A typically racist
Trib column might be: *France: The Foie Gras Years Are Over.*

Later there are the plucked fatty geese on TV, boy are they
plucked and fat. The livers come down a conveyor belt, thick, pasty
like the face of an American senator.

---

Everyone longs for the return of the witty aggressive man . . .
A dream. The witty aggressive man's back ransacking my
suitcase for drugs . . . But, he's so funny! *He's* a comedian.

And he wants a new wife an open marriage a threesome a foursome.

---

See this here gene? We'll take it out of those there
fat people, and put it in these here geese
so you won't have to feed them so much . . .
that way we're all gonna balance our budgets.

---

There is
a membrane I must
tear open, of

Your stupidity in me. Thousands
of centuries.

I don't believe anything You say (new folksong)

(Repeat)

Will not believe one thing I'm told or that I read.

(Repeat.)

_____

A peaceful moment,
foliage, a mountain slope.
I'm still wearing this damned white robe
lie down in grass. There's a bush with red berries

I still don't know why I'm creature . . .
evolutionary theory that dream bye bye

am not creature am not living
am not You.

_____

MESSAGE.

      inside this point
      a seed that grows in.

My middle finger's sore from too much up-pointing

# BEING WIGGY

in honor of the approaching
New Year:

    (Song . . . )

    All the dolls in the world
    given again for Christmas
    feel brand new having lunch . . .

    Oh, no, there isn't enough
    food.

Because down on Front Street, out on the street
in front of the old drugstore, tables
are set up on the pavement. My childhood girlfriends
sit at the tables, eating.
They look up, having finished, and say
That wasn't enough. Next I'm sitting there too
and we're asked if we want
the New New or   the New You.

---

More Christmas cards for breakfast
containing hardly any words . . .
a form of greeting just like
an academic poem. Definitely not the New You.

And here comes the New New,
in the same mail, yards of meringue
in white tome-like shapes . . .
light but pretending to be heavy.

Meister Eckhart says every day's Christmas
Christ being perpetually born in your soul's core.
In my soul's core, Eckhart, is a doll
so dark you can't find her eyes
from her in me I try to speak as outrageously as possible
because though there's enough food, there isn't enough
food.

"From the New New," a voice intones,
"will be eliminated.
I mean that in the New New
there will be no.
I mean that the New New
will be nothing but words."

I'm travelling with one of those actors or singers
talented but with a used-up face
for example, the late Roy Orbison
someone with wrinkles and a brunette wig, a pompadour, well
the point *is* that we're wearing brunette wigs, he and I
that's what we do; according to *me* we each have two
but according to *him* we have many more
identical brunette wigs that we wear.

The New You
arrives next Tuesday,
but one has never changed.

What do you think about destroying the rich
do you think we need their so-called talent
No. What about the people who hoard other things, like
notions of respectability, intellectuality . . .

Maybe it was Johnny Cash, in that dream,
what about his cash? destroy it but
get him to put on a wig and sing for us,
next Tuesday on New You's Day.

The New You is born within me every day—
the New You is real though often awful
the New New is empty material novelty
swamping and destroying personal essence
it seems to have that power
the triumph of the delusional if one
doesn't give into it isn't of one's
times, there's the danger of a brunette wig that's
mockable, old-fashioned . . .

Old Wig, says Hardwig.
Old Wig, but often true-blue.

---

What's born in one?
infinite universe
if not there where else
have you really located another place
born and born in
consciousness
to be much more than consciousness
more than a mammalian dream
it never dies in me

# EXPOSING MY BREASTS SO YOU'LL

are there
animals in E-
mail
if there is no?

Where does the animal
go?
that subject doesn't belong
here. Today
Sorry.

_____

My neighborhood in the 10th is sinking

the SNCF is constructing another RER line
the Eole, way below the *sous-sol*
a building has collapsed on the rue Papillon
'No evidence of anything to do with us
and our construction,' say the transport authorities
there's been a thudding audible for weeks
a low sort of DOOM   DOOM   DOOM.

_____

Where is the most negative
place I must pass through, Hardwill—

You're probably near the worst shit—

I'm not worthy, not me—

Just don't listen to anyone—now;
no man has anything to tell you—
and women, who's speaking really
I mean saying out.

The drunk suicide admires me
she's a brunette, by candlelight
she's never heard of the famous blonde
sitting next to me: I'm so pleased.

. . . later comes to life
on the canned goods side of
a department store:
young man, fully grown

more where that came from.

peeing in a chair is a symptom of what. There is no such thing
as a symptom.

Downstairs are rows and rows of people, in a
steamroom, all night. ignorant as hell,
a great big sexy party.

Different kinds of sex will create
a life story for You. You're
so pleased.

Don't you want a real job, You say to me
taking a break from the steamroom,
Or help, help the starving

and *never* make this statement
never say this for women

before ALL of the shit, the rest of
it rains on our heads.

Starving because there are "jobs" in our consciousness.

How can I hang up this third garment—
there are the other two—if I can't see what it is?

This is the problem with dreams, says Hardwood,
Your brain does it not your hands so it doesn't get done right.

I say, I can't even
make it appear. A jumper? Another damn dress?
There's always a third one, a third thing
What does *that* mean?

Duh, says Hardwood, Maybe, Honey
maybe it means there's more than two. A third
possibility.

———————————————

I dream I'll appear briefly onstage.
Should I expose my breasts
to call attention to our case?

———————————————

A blonde has written a letter with misspellings
but it could Help—she's a widow and so knows something—
but won't be fully attended to, a woman, wouldn't be
in waking life; many of my friends who are writers
wouldn't read it either. She isn't "educated" or liberal.
In my dream I'm trying to help her. It means that
I must go to the same stationery store twice,
hope I won't be seen going there again, repeating myself
unstylish, unoriginal.

———————————————

Mitch-ham says let's wear black
so any shit-splatters won't show up
in this shitty descent we've undertaken

his coat is long and dark
his hat broad-brimmed.

We're always under the arcade
by the merchandise, these days
these times

# IN THAT ROOM, IN THAT TIME, BUT LATER

the shit is the old
seems to be partly
the old Widow territory
Danger Waters, No

Danger pronounced with a hard gee like anger,
Dang her. Dang her waters. Hail,
Roger Miller, author of "Dang Me."

---

I've been through these death scenes too many times, Hardwood
I'll let one of the other widow-types do it

Her husband goes out the door with drugs in his pocket, says goodbye
to his father figure and dies. What's the point of my still caring about that

in a world of Real Hunger for Real Food?

---

Ice on the lake at the Buttes-Chaumont
yesterday; the swans had found
unfrozen water, stayed calm.
Someone had dropped a wrapped candy
Could I pick it up and eat it,
would it carry disease or be poisoned?
Stranger candy.
                A saint would taste it
just to see if she died. Catherine of Siena
drinking water that had washed
a woman's cancerous
ulcers of the breast.

---

Down in the caves,
the walls are black and dripping with ick.

I'm a poet I'll never be hungry. I don't care about
goddamned food. Uh uh, Hardfood says, You're checking
to see if you have enough tranqs
in case of a bereavement . . .

The whole world is eating. horrible
eating is horrible.

Eat this black bleck says Hardtimes
get you used to it, keep you alive down here
long enough to go down below
maybe even further below

below goddamned food, below food.

————————————————

We're in the shit-caves called The World.
There's a white pearl-like space mid shit, does one
stand there? I try it
does seeing the shit with detachment,
rather than being it, "help?"
I feel and look like a fucking statue—You might have to
stop swearing, says Hardwood, It's not
very literary    Mother FUCK I scream—
There is no language for this!!!

————————————————

This train I'm going to get on goes so fast
This train

This train I'm going to get on goes so fast
This train

This train I'm going to get on goes so fast
That the engineer, whom I know, is a nervous wreck

What train is it then? Oh it's the real Now Train
as opposed to the false Now Train

the There's-enough-time-to-fix-things false Now Train.

————————————————

"We're travelling over some more Danger Waters," says H,
"Of the variety we used to call bitter, now plain foul . . ."

Saintly-looking ghosts hover above the black ooze
they are Significant Individuals.
                                        I hate them. I say,

Who do they think they are, better food or something?

———————————————————

In so-called Dailiness (I once invented that usage)
an artisan, a jeweller, makes pretty garnet-beaded collars
near the Place des Vosges—
could go with a new perfume I'm imagining called Slavery.

But this is the French industrial base of which
I speak, edible fashion    it does create food.

———————————————————

New Year's Eve afternoon I ate a bad piece of *pâté de campagne*;
spent my Eve ill, threw up, no *champagne* . . .

———————————————————

Same old same old same, Hardwood.
It isn't the same, he drawls.

Why are you drawling?
I don't know, it seems "cultural," it seems like
I'm always being called on to be cultural . . .

it isn't the same now because
we went down lower. We're beginning to sound it.

———————————————————

International devourings of the hungry . . .
No world to be alive in yet I keep being here
throwing up, trying to eat again, writing
in my notebook 1996: that anyone is as
good as intelligent as talented as
the contents of their colon

# YOU COVER ALL THE WINDOWS WITH YOUR MANUSCRIPT PAGES

I'm failing again

when it's time, at a professional
luncheon—poets, publishers—
to recite the poem of another
(dead) poet: male after male
quickly does so without
prompting, takes me ages to catch on
to jump in and recite without being asked

all taking place in Needles, towards
the railroad tracks, on West Broadway.

As if that were the New York publishing world.

———————————————

A lovelier dream was of myself extending
     before me
into a geometry, a square with
just within its borders
a more delicately traced square.
Beside me was another being, a man
with the same extension
and in company we traversed the forest.

———————————————

Red flower, just one, in the canyon
next to cold noisy white and greenish stream.
There are no "senses"; there are intense manifestations
of absolute existence one is of and with,
                        Go on
into the cold stony cave,
wearing stiff boots. Mitch, let's talk—

(sound of water)
. . . aren't done with unpleasantness, babe, he says.

Nobody's ever called me Babe before, Unpleasantness Babe.

Can't it just be bloody eyeballs in the dark, so
I run, get in bed with you? Or
simple fear of my death.

The unpleasant truth is
I still *have* too much.

---

When You take off your No play mask,
You are a person, not a samurai; and that's worse . . .
You and I people in greedy houses . . .
a whole lower story of one of those modern
houses made of richly stained boards. Lots of plants
blue carpet, machines, matching dishes. This is very
       unpleasant . . .
it's the middle of the night, nothing moving,
idyllic leaves in moonlight outside, a garden,
      how creepy.

---

I've been sleeping very twitchily—

A man crowded me, last night, on a train, in a dream
Stretched into my seat to sleep: I yelled and he backed off.

Another showed me letters full of names of current poets
I said I hated that stuff all that naming.
How can you hate a name like Burns-Cherry? he said,
Just the name itself is wonderful.
Aw, I know all that stuff already, I said, all that word stuff.

I do. I already know all that word stuff.

I pursue You through small
boxy corridors, intricate recesses,
in the form of a spirit—
You are trying to escape and not face me but
especially not to awaken.

Now You are two men
You weigh me
I weigh 48 pharns and phorns
What does that mean
You refuse to explain    or to convert
my weight into pounds
Your measure, You imply, is absolute.

———————————

I still have too much. A large black closet for example
and underwear scattered on a carpet
I have personal style: I still have too much.

And
a *carte bleue*. And not equality

will die unequal.
I'm charged with never forgetting that.

———————————

A poetry world over there
a muted reading at night in a bookstore
I have to read for these people. Talk to a woman with
long hair. Doesn't really care
about poetry, cares about herself, her
little poems. Everything's amateurish, scaled down.

I crave your presence Mitch

## WILL DIE AND DIE IN SO MANY WAYS, AS PROFESSIONAL AND CULTURAL ENTITY

suddenly in childhood room
in my mind, in bed there:
by holding on to
past innocence, get
around the necessity of changing

in relation to what I *have*
now? No. No.
How am I going to change?
I don't know. Have to.
Mirror of poem.

---

A woman—whom on awakening
I know was the Bionic Woman—
is photographing herself repeatedly, obsessively.
She says she assumes that inside she's encrusted
with layers of cancer. This photography is actually
a self-given cancer treatment:
I'm irradiating the cancer, she says.
But this is dangerous; and she hasn't been diagnosed;
I seem to be in a point-of-view that's alarmed—
a group point-of-view—she's likely
to kill herself with her so-called treatment.

---

A dead speedfreak and I
are standing in a hotel lobby—
I associate it with Phoenix—
the hotel clerk we're speaking to
is a keeper of mental quickness or universal energy.
"Don't get too near
the sources of speed!" I say jokingly
to the speedfreak. He laughs.

that's
the same warning, society's warning: Don't try to get
too close . . . too close to origin
we as we make us are all
all you should think about. Stay in hell.

---

Down, down.

Sun rays around the dark face.
Wearing a white bathrobe,
sit on a lawn. version of the Golden City
how we can live together: in a sanitorium.
What does the Company *do?* of Good People.
Why do I dislike the idea
of the benign and altruistic friends:
I'm going to reject this city for a different vision.

---

. . . in the canyon. A tunnel extends
below the bottom of the canyon
and Hardwood is there in khaki
at the tunnel's rim. We climb down—
am I myself or Jane Russell
that arch-brunette, in *Foxfire*. Dissolves

I'm only a light, in the darkest of rooms,
a heatless candle glow
in Mitch-ham's hand. "It isn't particularly good,
it isn't particularly social. Still,
it's transcendent,"
he says, with a shrug.

Mark this event with an asterisk.

---

Wrenchingly back at life.
At an opening, a Frenchwoman
tells me how terrible the French are
I don't agree.
I look for the light she is—sour

the world takes place for her forever
pickle-flavored, pucker-mouthed.
I'd told her I was a poet
she told me that was cute: *Mignon.*

———————————

Boring
        speaking of light
just a way of
talking. Language,
oh god who cares.
                        A precise-
brained poet ambles near.
run away . . .

He's not as precise as
one might think

he grooms his mind with a sponge,
soaks up all the new theory
then squeezes
the tepid liquid onto his head.

Now, grovel before him,
he thinks! He thinks!
Just look how he drips with water
all by himself!

———————————

Can't remember the damn dream.
It was a tall woman from another planet
with badly cut bangs. There were two of her,
one on the other planet and one here.
From the bangs I'd say she's me. definitely.

———————————

Down here there's always a light breeze.

Here comes my drunken
Hardwill, you genius.

He says, There's a place where new knowledge
stops, where knowing has resounded back to the beginning.
Then it is what it is and there isn't any more.
There isn't always more.
There is such a thing as absolute definition;
that's what I've just detected.
*You* are absolute . . .
I, myself, I say.
Yes

He's speaking in his younger movie voice
his whisky clinks

# DO I HAVE TO BE MAD NOW LATER AND ALWAYS

morning, a bouquet of open *oeillets*—
being a member of a dying but still selfish race . . .
No, am a spiritual tough-girl;
a member of many selfish races:
pigheaded You.

---

Wish I had never
learned anything—

   Will I
know Your inculcations
when I'm dead?

am supposed to give
You even more than
the self You've already
taken, keep serving
You.

---

Hardwood, come here

    I'm
crying, a soul, down in some valley
I want to talk *my* language

So, give, says H.

. . . trash all the hookers,
I know so many. Or love the
scrofulous artisans
of a country's values where
you live is what you are

no escapees; I detest
their house and car
their pretentious
sexualities . . .
cure the sexist mess with abortion,
macho with barbarism . . .
I am those things.

I think you're a spiritual baglady now, says Hardwood.

I can't control my lips . . .

Ugly soul, a soul's the universe's asshole
that's why everyone denies it.

———————————————

I was in two places at once,
two parties in two houses with two "boys"

Consciousness and unconsciousness ever
where is a thirdness?

Later,
Ursula Andress was posing
nude again for a magazine
though "old": overly made up . . .
she shouldn't pluck her eyebrows

she holds up a baby against her nude body—
From inside a hot-tub, I make a telephone call . . .

———————————————

Later, sink down in soul. No, can't.

Apocalypses are commonplace, really,
especially if you're in one
I don't have to list them, at least a score
in the last fifty years and You think such
a vision of the century, of the future is extreme?
What else is going on?

Oh beautiful, a red butterfly
on my dusky soul-shoulder
I'm posing for the soul centerfold now
covered strategically as they say with more and more
blood-red butterflies. I look pissed-off
that's mistaken for sultry. I am Arsenal Undress
and I will blow your mind to pieces
if I just can. If You come one step closer
with any more Ideas.

I'm blowing up my own mind

I saw Mitch-ham in
one of my favorite
macho-movies Sunday night

kill some guys, make some jokes, very friendly;
the villain is allowed a death scene
in a passage of quiet mannerliness

who's ever cared about the corpses—
the Imagination and the Real World
are never the same now are they . . .

strew your works with purely symbolic "bodies"
dead or alive, write a book on de Sade

I haven't any Real idea who I am
or where I live
in this moment.

In a make-enemies phase which
ones should you choose—
I choose You because
You're still not sick of Yourself.

When the bloody butterflies
fly away, says Hardwood,
Will we be able to see the details
of the soul's body?
One lives for that, to "see"
death from the inside out.

Look it's some talking pills
Should I take that one? It's called a "dos"
but it might be a "sod"

be a woman, it says, take your hormones
you know your "gender" (I'm not
a word, I say, though you are a pill)

And when the bloody butterflies fly off
and when the bloody butterflies fly off

But You, You wouldn't
recognize it

# LOST THE PLUMBING LOST MY STORY GOOD

our galaxy is shaped like a doughnut,
they say, with a black-hole center—
would there be such a thing as a "black-hole center"
if You weren't alive?

                                    I play back all
my messages on my answerphone—
they are pictorial: in one a woman
accidentally reveals her naked crotch.
                                    Erase that message
not a proper black hole, someone says.

————————————————

I'm not existing this minute

Hardtime says, You can't say that.
Anyone can say anything, I say. They
do all the time: that souls are reincarnated,
that Christ rose from the dead, that
I am exactly material and in fact non-
existent as a self, am everyone else.
No one's here

no one's responsible
for the fact that Your bank account's
larger than another's. Or that
our society
routinely exploits other ones

It's the government!

Naw, by that definition there's no government either.

My plumbing is now leaking in my upper story
no it's worse it's completely ripping out of the wall
room's filling with water.
A pedestrian experimental prose writer
advises me to send a large bill for the damage
to a gossip columnist.

Why would I bill a gossip columnist? I ask Hardwood.
The prose version, he says, is
responsible for your whole mess
it built the bad plumbing. If the prose writer
blames the plumbing's failure
on simple prose (gossip, folk tales) he (the futurist intellectual)
can't be guilty . . .

The international prose version states
that we are all
employees. Non-selves

Poetry is maintained secretly
on an individual basis
in Your dreams at night

Large dark house.
For artistic and philosophical and political
purposes I'm naked.
Lying on the couch like a model.

Visited a French friend an artisan
a socialist, she despised the strike
it robbed her of three months' revenue
in her small business—she's a seamstress.
The *cheminots* are pigs: their union
added to a life already rather hard—that is
she arrives at her atelier at seven and
         works till seven—
an hour of walking, each way, for three and a half

weeks.
And no one's buying yet, who can afford to?

––––––––––––––––––––––––––––

I have an important dream

we're among tropical plants, Hawaii
in the Seventies, posing for photos.
My sister holds so still that a large butterfly
brown and beautiful, has landed on her shoulder.
My father says, We need someone in a halo now.
I'll sit in one, I say—meaning thrust my ass through one,
sounds like a joke—I think to myself, They don't know
that I'm going to do just that. Naked. They won't approve.

This has been the project of my life.

      Later on a storm is coming—men outside the house
      women inside, other side of the window,
      behind the glass though exactly back of the men
      no a little below them, a split-level house, so behind their asses—
      'We should at least be able to touch them,' we say
      but we can't, there's glass between.

. . . This brown butterfly's the world's
most beautiful butterfly.

If we could get rid of brain-based worth,
establish ass-based worth? then

we would be spiritual equals.

It's as if we're not even invented. We've missed it so far.

Living holds still for a moment, wearing
its soul on its sleeve,
though there's a war near this dream.

My dreams are parables to myself
from the message-leaver in the caves

FIND YOUR ASS
FIND YOUR WIT
FIND YOUR SANCTITY

Hardwood tries to photograph
the now quick-flitting brown butterfly
"It's you," he says, "it's you"

# OH PUT SOME OBSCENELY CONCRETE NOUNS BACK IN YOUR POEMS

the house full of
garbage is on fire,
a new house made
of blonde wood. The
father our teacher is sleeping.
Wake him up and tell him,
get a bucket, I
say to small children.
I was trying
to clean up the pizza boxes
and crumpled pages of typing when
the outside corner of the house
caught on fire again.

---

In nearby fantasy, dark figures
slump brooding. Will I
change enough before I die?
The reason I'm important is that You're doomed
i.e. I must be I not U oh eek ah yes,
vowels . . . beloved of poets,
the ones who don't love to talk about
syntax, absence, desire, localism
all the irrelevancies

Localism's a nice idea
when all your clothes, food, objects
are produced down the street.
A poem for my
audience: dealing with our
concerns: that's a good one.

---

A navel-like dark pool of water
sit down at, in caverns.
Cerebral council. Mitch sits down.

Perhaps, I mean maybe, I say,
at bottom we think within pictures
in a dreaming underneath mind always going on.
It supports words.

He gives me an amused look, smoking
He's smoking, not drinking, lately.

Splash feet in water.

He scratches his neck.

This is a break. Being tranquil

You and I talking, here,
are like that thinking, he says.

Not dissimilar, I say. We're in
a tableau that's alive and moving within itself . . .
producing my "thoughts."

———————————————

My sister life keeps arriving
or trying to take off in dreams.
In the Eurostar Station
there are planes and trains for all the major cities . . .

This tier of life's a croissant-zone, so clean,
so full of the sense one is someone

Otherwise further below,
below the shit walk through flames.
They wave like orange pampas grass
dry and there's no other food.

———————————————

There's a bloody wristbone in the mud
on TV in Srebrenica.
My life—not my self—isn't real. What
would make it so.
I'm not sure anymore.
I have love, I know love, that's not the answer.
We need to be rational, deeply logical
in a way that pours outwards whatever the cost
to our power, self-esteem, and emotional satisfaction.

———————————————

Descend descend descend—I do that in all my poems
Where's Hardlife? I search for him between the cottony flames . . .

There's Mitch and Opaquesoul
in the flames, both in black.
She shimmers out of sight,
like a heat mirage, at my approach.

Lay yourself on the line, he says.
Right there.

A black line among orange-red flutters.
I lie down on it

part lips to speak:
When I was united last night asleep
I lived in a creation beneath
verbal thinking, that was whole and seemed
uncreated

Can you will me a definition of dreams?

Speaking, he says, as your detective
dreams are the deepest way of thinking
maybe the first way of thinking.
They come towards the soul from its secret
inventing life, scaring you shitless
and probably trying to tell you about
that secret

## HEALTHY AND FOOLISH THE MAINSTREAM STARS OF KNEEJERK JOY AND DESPAIR MAY WIN THE FUTURE

but now, now
it's so hard to work for
history . . .
What kind of, or is there, a future?
Or, with so many names
crowding us in new technologies
for printing and hyping
books, why shouldn't the best be lost?
One may be smarter than history, forever,
as one's smarter than the media, or the University.

_____

Fifteen houses on a certain street in a certain town in the Jura
have caught on fire—this in the last three months.
The EDF—the French gas & electric—
and the Devil have been previously blamed.
The Devil's also said to be active in the Pyrenees.
But now an alleged *pyromane* has been arrested;
he'd previously been questioned in connection with
the conflagration of his own closet. He
called the fires inexplicable, supernatural.

_____

Reviewing this poem: goes to the left, Dante, etcetera.
That was a long time ago now
too much to recapitulate too much living twisting informal detail.

Going left go green go green
"You have a
case of green light," says a voice.
Now the body of a man on the ground
near halted car: someone hurt

by a woman's green-light driving . . .
Green light, in his ear
green light, in his ear always: thinks he's
going, can't hear her car coming.
It was her
green light.

———————————————

Johnny Cash's hundred-year-old face
consisting of a large nose sings:
"I fell in-
to a burning ring of fire . . ."

———————————————

"If you keep talking like this you'll hurt someone":
that voice again the Be-Nice voice.

———————————————

Be nice to the Le Pen-ite from Marseilles
who'll give you a good price for the moving job,
I was; and the woman who asked me if my poem,
months later anthologized in the Norton, wasn't just notes for a poem;
the man who groped me, the one who slapped my ass,
and all the men in the last three years, poets and journalists themselves,
who have never so much as acknowledged that
I might have a profession at all, much less be a writer too

Be Nice
Be Nice . . .

I blow my nose over all of you,
this be-colded fiery day in February.

Back to my flames.

———————————————

Dreamed of a poetry sect again
it was associated with two kinds of lettuce,
        tiny heads
of lettuce: one white, one yellow-edged

          like endive
though I thought it was miniature bok choy . . .

Maybe lettuce is Lutèce, Paris. Maybe.
Or maybe just a perpetual 'Let us.'

I sit
still
flames
cover
me.

_____

But in my so-called death, a dream
there must be a lot of people who . . .

_____

Dark but light-eyed, huddled near a rock
I almost knew something but
knowledge comes in bits, cumulatively,
enmeshed in tableaux,
in dreams for example or poems or, in life,
events in a room for awhile.
The units of time are tableaux.

_____

Hardwood, in my dream a voice said the following,
"Unlike our parents the panthers . . ."

Yes, he says, Yes, unlike our parents the panthers
we don't spring on our prey with our whole selves
        Any
technology these days
is better than a body or a self—
How's your burnt
panther soul today?

I and panther spiritual equals

will never be friends.

And I and You?

In these tableaux experience consists of—
in these tableaux.

The man's face was burnt beyond all recognition
on the *policier* "Navarro" last night.
He was a rich artist, he abused his daughter, he owned a Delacroix.
They kept playing oogly boogly spook music in the background . . .
'Happy Birthday, Chief!' that's the surprise party
for Navarro . . . He's a policeman, not
a *séropositif* artist;
his daughter isn't even
on the pill.

———————————————

Below the flames might be crystal?
what the fuck good would that be

# IT'S DUMB TO BE A MEMBER OF A DOMINANT SPECIES

snow falling outside the window of Procope
on windowbox paperwhite narcissus—
it stops. What language were they speaking
at the next table? I don't know

Diderot, Robespierre, and Nazis have eaten here
Silver lines impinge on the scene
invisible connections to the past and the future
the room on the second floor is rooted

in the first floor, the wine cellar, tribal dreams
such as the union of egg and sperm, the existence
of a monster like a man or a woman
the necessity of killing and of its regulation
the dream—the tribal dream—is of food and sex
after having destroyed the enemy.

———————————————

World passing by in tableaux
forming from and dissolving back to
waves or clouds . . .

The pouches under Mitch-ham's eyes are so large
I'm tempted to poke them with a hatpin
and see what comes out. Liquid crystal he says or ichor,
not pus or tears—

a weak shower of spermlike snow
falls on our flames . . .

REJOICE IN THE INIQUITIES OF THE LORD

BUDDHA PRACTICES AUTOFELLATIO

MOHAMMED IS A MUGGER

such are the messages
left on the walls
just visible through fire

WE LIVE IN MYTHOLOGY BUT MYTHS ARE STUPID

THE HEART SINKS LIKE A STONE MYTH

THE SCIENTIFIC METHOD IS ONLY
THE MYTH OF THE SCIENTIFIC METHOD,
WHICH WILL EVAPORATE WITH THIS CIVILIZATION

MITCH-HAM IS A MYTH

ANY PEOPLE'S WAYS ARE TOTALLY
OFF THE WALL, THIS WALL.

———————————————

I'd like to find the humility room,
I say, though humility's a myth—

It's simply, again, says Mitch,
the room where other people starve, not a myth.

———————————————

Went to a restaurant once more. Ate a duck. Guilt.

———————————————

I dream I pull down from the sky
yards and yards of
a mesh-like silver-grey
narrow band of a fabric,
with a purse attached.
And a newspaper.
In a young tribal society

this might become the story
of how we got our ways,
receiving from heaven
our wealth and
the first great length of our
headband and belt material;
we could organize a festival
where it fell from
the sky every year
as in the beginning
and we danced, holding
the ribbon high over our heads.

_____

I'm eating   her   food.

_____

I can have any books I want from this box . . .

One's about foretelling the future from clouds,
a practice apparently found in many cultures:
Australian Aboriginal, Amer-Indian, African, etc.
Clouds are observed and painted with
unadulterated pigments in broad brushstrokes

e.g. several crimson swaths against a grey-blue mass
which subtly changes across its grainy swelling;
color renders volume and depth and the stratification
of the clouds—maybe the future's told from those qualities.
The future being ominous . . . that's the drift of this book.

_____

A conversation. "I'm waiting for . . ."
a myth of rescuing the future

We sanction no war whatsoever
just or unjust.
As a matter of fact we do nothing
we use no more fuel, drive no more cars
because we have tied our hands

with the silver-grey fabric.
It's hard to eat, hard to write. Our enemies
can kill us if they want.
I think they're us anyway
and we were already doing that, killing us
if we wanted

## PEOPLE COULD LIVE IN THIS TOWN, THEY DON'T BUT I'M GOING TO

parking a neon-lit
go-green truck

in a basement
lit itself by go-green neon . . .

I'm having truck now with this
low-down basement

"I've planted my butt here below,
below the flames in a dry

earthen Rational Room. It's very
very calm," Hardwood says.

This is the new empty house
where I hear war over there.

There's always some war.

―――――――――――――

Darkly she's wearing the long Stop-red coat she recently
posed in for the newspaper—one like *The Daily Mail*
with a color photo—

Valentine Soul—
stop with me.

Truth courses through the body
I feel it.
The balm
coursing through me.

It's not words or love.
It hasn't ever been defined.

*Well I'm indigenous*
Of course.

---

Walking in a field
a man in jeans I'm him his legs
That's because I am soul
and could almost be anyone's

Up to the point where he
does anything in particular. Thinks
the next thing . . .

I once dreamed I was not myself
was a woman in a plain grey dress
married to an alcoholic slick-haired man we lived
in a bare clean apartment I've
rarely felt such pain—it wasn't so much what the life was like

it was that I was inhabiting another person.

---

In life I've signed a petition
against the café downstairs those noisy bastards:
this is the common good.

A short feisty big-nosed woman
her hair stuffed into a newsboy's cap
gets on métro, announces she's sick
has a child and they're sleeping on the street.
Everyone's deciding whether or not they believe her
such a big deal this belief for two francs
I mean if you believe in the Virgin Birth
or in Progress or Supply-side economics.

In long black cloth again veil or shroud is it
lying on my belly on the ground
the tableaux come from below here, just below do they
how can I find their source when I'm always in one
is their source one

I sit up and push this shit off my head

I'm wearing jeans and a brown sweater now
I'm in the past again, empty habit, this outfit.

The terrible face of that Forbes man
like when you play Mr. Potato Head
with your Mom's same old wrinkled potato.
All those fucking guys, again
they don't look like anyone I know
or like anyone I grew up with
They don't even look like a woman.
Dole doesn't look as much
like The Dark Emperor this year,
well not next to Buchanan's
malicious Irish eyes
What are we doing—*we're* doing it, not them—
in every country I can think of
Chirac that shit-eating look, but John Major's
the shoddiest.

Dreamed the street artist's talent,
at Les Halles, was to make
a big purple wig. Yarn dreads
in an 18th Century arrangement.
Some demented woman behind me
indicated I must worship, even wear
this new atrocity;
another impossible heavy head.

There is a sort of crystal. & I've
said so before. It's the rationality
I've been speaking of
sometimes I perceive it as a coursing soul-liquid
sometimes as an air that I'm in
somewhat thick with blue glints.
I experience it literally

## MY HAIR IS TERRIBLY DIRTY AND THE
## DRESS LOOKS DRAB

the Buttes shut, full of snow.
Run around the periphery
and then find out that Buchanan has won in New Hampshire.
Black ice across Europe; dream of Bob Dole all night—
he says he's changing and that his poems prove it,
all near the Botzaris métro stop with green trees.

———————————————

The Bob Doll and Mrs. Bob Doll
discuss why *she* can't be President:
because, he says, This is My Big Opportunity.
Later she finds Jesus, prays to the faroff Jesus doll
on the shelf above the Presidents.
Above the Presidents.

———————————————

What a horrible place, dirty mental black space
that I'm in—suddenly outside of it I close it:
it's a shiny silver
some sort of oven with knobs,
a little like the food materializer
on the old Star Trek.
What was I doing in there?
I can't tell you. Though my rule for this poem
is honesty, my other rule is Fuck You.

———————————————

There are people in the caves today walking up and down
in black, like clerics. The French bishops
have taken the stand that condoms
may now be used against AIDS; this means
these guys in black are tiptoeing cautiously
into my actual psyche, getting more normal, a little.

Mitch-ham's dressed as the preacher
in *Night of the Hunter*.
No he isn't.
That was a flash hallucination.
He's wearing a casual shirt and khaki pants.

Is there a message:

"dripping dropping drugs of stone policy . . ."

_____

They're lifting their ban
on the New York School
and the so-called name-dropping . . .

Khruschev, Beckett, a Puerto-Rican cab-driver,
Vincent—this mentioning of people

as if they existed . . .

_____

Leaving New York, every night
and the room's getting emptier, the contents
of the boxes and files are mostly selected now:
in this white-walled room like a stateroom
across the water, at twilight, from the skyline.

You, my You with a capital Y,
You are transnational, here, anywhere. Someone in the corner
up on the top bunk of the stateroom.

_____

. . . a story taking place in a beach town
in relation to a restaurant two-story glass-fronted

A customer, a woman in a turquoise bikini,
has been murdered because she's a woman.
        The manager,
a dirty blonde man in a hibiscused Hawaiian shirt,
will take another poll of his customers

to see how sexist they still are.
                              I'm walking
in the downtown area myself, it's full of cotton
windblown in everyone's eyes. But the cotton
is really cotton centers. Why is that?

I mean small black-lined flower centers
that are left when the cotton is gone . . . the brains of
the fertility.
The brains of the fertility.

What's left after she's murdered. Myself at this age.

_____


The function of poetry has changed so much—
doesn't tell stories, instruct, is not recited as rite,
does not distill the people's wisdom
or even prophesy much. What does it
do then?

What are You doing?

_____


That small one-story house
again, in a field
I'm there with others . . .

Maybe it's Dorset. Gunshots.
One of us is a nurse. But I have
a different useful skill

# MEET ME AT LA CHAPELLE FOR SOME MORE SALAMI

I tell the Mafia don, the old man, I'm looking for my mother—

"No one ever sits down with me for myself," he says

Then, "There's a hit tonight
you can take part in."
                        I do, I have,

in an instant, in the next tableau
he and a boy from a TV show
are dead, shot up, blood streaming.

Everyone admires me for my participation in this hit.

_____

Grey pâté sky. République

Cops everywhere. Some druggy people;
and peasantlike people: woman, toothless, in scarf
not a gypsy, and one-legged old man, crutch
argue with métro maintenance worker. Cops
run past them: it's somewhere else,
what they're running to

I would possibly prefer death to another accordionist.

_____

Can't EVER get the clothes right this skirt
goes all the way to the ground
pleated in shiny taffeta
I'm too tired to change, so

I will wear it down into the caves of my
true love, so rational—

in this room there is a rug a picture on
the wall a few books.

Hardwood yawns

the room darkens and I write
"beyond fifty I'm sinking."

      Then
"from the Secret:
Abolish these categories of pain
(or is it love)
Let it all be one pain
Pain swallows itself, dies like a star."

I don't love, not towards You
but it's possible just to love, towards no one,
like a cat.

Later I sit intimately
with a man, a Mitch-like shadow.
We melt together becoming the center of a flower
the black center of a huge    fuschia-colored blossom—
the so called code? is a form of love . . .

_____

*Mes amis, mes très chers amis,*
I am remembering how to be a jerk
from the deepest recesses of my DNA echoing corridors so
you won't lose this great folk art:
How to be obnoxious, to shit in a scientist's hat . . .

What else know? I hope, *mes chers amis,*
that before you die you've looked
some god in the eye and said NO.

That's what Hardwood
has said today.

These dioramas illustrating my poem are beautiful
these coconut-shell-like structures are caves, these photos
of what happens—next to the words—are also the words.
When I look at the illustrations such
richly textured assemblages—foil, bark, jewels—I hear
the words as if read aloud; but
that's like what reading really is. Or is thinking
like that? No of course not, thinking wasn't
previously made; and one's emotions course through
the diorama one's in when thinking,
making it tremble—the words often garble
or aren't words at all but illuminations, tiny doorways of light.


In this TV show, German, a middle-aged hostessy
very intelligent—the police inspector says so—
                high school teacher
murders her student, an adolescent male. That's
                pretty funny, heavily.
Not anyone's mother, she's in love
with a different boy with unblinking round blue eyes.
Oh really


You are the sufferer.
I carry the corpse, carry
the dead weight for you;
but he's your father
not mine. That was one dream, remember?

There's a baby who
has somewhat perhaps
of an old man's bald head and
wears glasses.
He has flower parts for a nose,
stamens and such:
I hold his head very tenderly
to my naked chest. That's another

## BUT MY REAL DREAMS ARE OBJECTIVE (OBJECTS MADE OF ME BY THE SECRET)

make this lighter, light as a
lighter
club.

_____

World saturated with estrogen
so where's our Mother.
This article says we don't know if our water
contains significant birth-control-pill residue

I used to take those things
Last night in my dreams, I took downers though,
pills that made the muscles feel ethereal
in Needles, at night, walking on Bailey Avenue . . .

_____

Slipping down a dark vertical tunnel
into a darker . . .
                    (shrill bird outside, there, in Paris)

climbing down.
Past mesa with small white pueblo,
obsidian sheer cliff blood-streaked.
I'm just sliding no ladder

and I land at
the bottom, eyes closed, delicate
membranes of lids sticky shut.
I'm dormant, cicadalike, sweet . . .
is there always
a place in the universe
to land when you

fall off or out of
your life—

an abstraction holds this cicada bundle
a mothering line, curved, holds
the new entity.

A new kind of mother. Holding me.
Quietly, this is important.

—————————————————

This flow, this flow, does it have a particular
emphasis or shape, glints all similar
in ruffled liquid (laced with chemicals).

—————————————————

The French medical bureaucracy
wants to abort more Down's Syndrome babies.

Who do You think
should have been aborted?
instead of the people who were . . .

Perhaps my new rebirth
should have been aborted. Too late;
the lovely line mother the abstraction who holds
me, hovers, bent, near.

—————————————————

I've had, for some fifteen years, a desire to be
"reborn." The terminology, the specifics of the wish,
may come from my evangelical background;
the impulse more generally comes from my disgust
and fatigue with the world I'm given, as elucidated
in this poem.
              Can personal transformation,
uninvolved with established hierarchies, actual (religion)
or ideal (books), be achieved?

But it never happens all at once, rather
is fitful, regressive, prolonged, even lifelong,
though occasionally hurtles me, for a moment,
into a different future.

---

The line-mother holds me, geometry-mother
tender and stark.
I think this may be happening
all the time.

---

Dreamed of a paranoid felon
I used to know years ago, a masculine
soul in black glasses whom I think
I may have failed—can't really remember.
I myself was in a state when he wrote and asked me
to check on something . . . people were stealing
his poems from his safety deposit box, while he
was in a top-security psychiatric prison, would I go get them?

He was obviously correct in some way

where are Your poems

I don't want him to see me
I walk past rows and rows of shellfish
as stealthily as possible. He sits nearby.

---

Any American poet is an American poet.

Any poet is a poet.

---

I've forgotten all about
my new birth

# DON'T GIVE ME DROVEL, GIVE ME A SHOVEL
## (POPULAR POEM)

any living tableau
contains much that we know
of how to make a world
how to combine
dream and planet, personal
and communal
dreams with the reality of geology
and those who don't dream with us,
animals and plants.

I'm glad it doesn't all dream with me.

Why can't You respect
those that You don't dream with.

———————————————

Something brown is falling from
the heavens; one of my little
grandma's favorite expressions:
"Well, shit on you!"

It stopped. Out the window.

———————————————

There was this party and it was also a small swimming pool,
so I swam a few laps but the room was too small, full
of poets chatting. The young ones, beautiful, pretentious,
wear garlands in their hair. The new young-poet
sexuality is threesomes . . . but right now, they're writing.
The silky-bearded male writes his poems in ancient Greek
and hands them to either the blonde girl or the redhead for praise . . .
the redhead herself being well-published, by Westphalian Press.

"My name," she says, "is Donna Ye-Yeats."
She awaits more approval and gets it. She's very beautiful.

---

Woman in populous room, emaciated, naked
hands me a plump nude male baby.

        I can't look at her
she's so thin—
       Maybe
she's starved for something: A new
politics. Or poetry. Both
One can't exist without the other.

---

A large dog, Sirius—
I don't know what kind of dog dogs are—
walks toward moon. Big
moon blotting out horizon

Hardwood says, That moon
is whose soul. The soul of Sirius.

I had thought it was mine.

---

Write as if left-handed:
        Soul says
Carry my bucket. Help me scrub the floor
the room is Blank, goes blank on me
I don't know what it is, this room, but we must wash the floor.
It's the only floor that needs to be clean,
the only floor in the world that really needs to be clean.
And we don't need to hire somebody else to do it.

. . . Needs to be clean
I would rather mop a floor
than wear this dress I get paid for,
teaching in hell
how to win.

---

Where do the poor go for help?
They go to the poor.

---

Tremendous selfishness to get even.
Well I wouldn't let them walk on me.
Not as a woman. But
I want You to enter

this tableau where there's nothing to lose
because one has nothing. A clean floor.
I don't even have to win the argument,
which was based on Having, too. Having a point-of-view.

---

X now lives in a huge apartment with a blonde.
We might have been rich together!
A penthouse with a garden of pheasant-
and guinea-fowl-feathered
plants . . .

Later I'm walking on 14th Street, New York
in the Paladium block
pushing a package on luggage wheels.
Another woman's involved and we've
pushed it backwards forwards
"I've even shot it," she says.
We still can't get it to the event
which used to be some kind of festival
but is now just a lecture with snow on the ground.

Suddenly at the Paladium, dancing poets performing . . .
limited vocabs: the supposition
is that The People—someone keeps pointing to audience—
have limited vocabularies, do re mi.
The People themselves assume
that poetry has a limited vocabulary, that that
is the form, as is the simple-minded
psychology of these "popular poets":
they must make The People cheer. Okay, The People cheer

# OPEN-STOMACH WOMAN

wooden chair, earth wall and floor
Mitch in his black preacher clothes pushes big hat back—
Doll, opaque Doll, in a rocking chair, in a granny dress

You guys are, like, my ancestors now?

They ain't answerin.

She rocks, he lifts a bottle of whiskey and glugs one.

———————————————

To the right of "to make it"
is a hook, labelled
HANG UP YOUR CHANGE. STOP HERE.
My change is a frayed black silk scarf
bordered with flat red roses . . .
I don't hang it up yet

I go to the left . . . follow
a succession of doormats outside to a field
No one there. No one there again.

———————————————

*Newsweek* arrives shrieking
French culture is now street culture, American-style.
This is good.

Colonize me baby, Hardwood says.

I pass on by him in the high school auditorium

I sit down next to an American poet
to collaborate on a poem and she

turns to me and says, "Hello, Ninotchka!"
Oh yes, I think, that was always the diminutive of Notley.

am the enemy Russian
or is it defector,
have defected from our heart.

---

This mimeo rag from the 70's
edited by 19-year-old nobody
whom we used to know
now sells for 40 dollars

I suppose we're in it
we who're lying on the sidewalk.
One of us, the dead one,
says to the girl selling it—
who's mostly a big coat—
"You're the enemy!"
He says this good-naturedly.

Who is she? That woman from 10,000 Maniacs
once sang in a coat on TV

Maybe it's her. Half-assed art.

---

Yes I think there could be new definitions
of art, sexuality, politics, the sacred, social relations—
they may even be "evolving" right now
especially in some privileged countries.
Overall, the planet seems to be dying;
everyone has a bomb;
genocidal processes have been stepped up.

---

Mitch spits on the porch.
I'm in the Doll's chair.
When you die, he says, it's just you.

I'm not ragged, I say. I'm a whole soul.
An ecstatic microbe.

We are both suddenly deep deep down
in a melting black velvet
there's a gas lamp right there
some of its rays are white and some of them yellow.

We sit down by the table it rests on—
the Coleman lantern—
on folding chairs.

Silence. Crystalline.

_____

It's tiring to abolish
ten thousand years of tradition
in order to live a life,
be a functioning "woman" poet.

The poles are melting.

I might think to end this whole work
if I'd said that five hundred times
but not if I've said it fifty . . .

I have my own rules here.

_____

I dream I'm sharing a yellow cab
with an "open-stomach" woman:
you can see the orderly contents
of her midriff
behind plastic

I will get out of the cab first
she will go on, carry on

I awaken with the phrase
"open-stomach woman"

repeated in my head
like the chorus of a rock song

I will now have to posit
The Open-Stomach School of Poetry

# LEVELING

*(MARCH 10, 1996–JUNE 17, 1996)*

# I KNOW YOU'LL MAKE FUN OF THE CLOTHES THE MAGI ARE WEARING

these three dark women I know
arrive at the party dressed in turbans
they shake my hand
I'm afraid people will make fun of them

the house is a city, it's stated the time's
The Real Sixties that we've gone literally
into the past of people making revolution
i.e. struggling for some flat silver jewelry

I worry about girlchild dead in the future
can't seem to find her in the past at the party
a lone woman whose name means poet
measures lengths of telephone wire blissfully

The white poet of Whitewake Avenue
that hermetic suburb
wants attention for *his* poetry
keeps holding up the map of *his* neighborhood

If this is really a revolution,
shouldn't everybody be here?
Is everybody who ever lived here? or will live,
here
a place for everyone.

———————————————

Deep caves

What I am being is not from a source but is it.

Of tableaux,
could there be a template tableau
one dies into forever?

A decision how to live.
I can't find the right words for it yet.

———————————————

Little boy says of girls, "Now
they're pity, aren't they?"

Pity's so different from pretty but
just as allegorical. Girls are
still that function. All the men the male leaders
of the world are swaggering
in Egypt right now
at the anti-terrorist convention.

———————————————

Come across a definition of the concept "society"
which contains the notion that a "society"
considers the welfare of each individual therein—
a laugh. Then

I dream that a brunette I know, younger,
more slender than in life,
has been unhappy but now, better,
performs a long poem, at night,
outside an old stone church with yellow-lit windows

ivy on the church    sturdy tables and
chairs in this churchyard

with place settings on the tables:
at each place, she sings a line of the poem.

It provides for anyone who sits down

That is how to live, singing that poem.
Living, singing that poem.

———————————————

At dinner with some people with
an unhealthy fear of poverty . . .

The gist is we can't join the poor, they must join us.
They    must change    Not us
We can't sink towards them
Won't even meet them halfway.
As we must.

―――――――――――――――――

Some-one
will have to give up power
some-time . . .

I gave it all to drink
er, in a former life, says Hardwood

I gave up power to a thing like drink
there's something to be said for that

a harmless addict. Not a president
or leader.

―――――――――――――――――

Down.

babble low long time Rio Grande

eagleheaded yelloweyed capewinged presence . . .

Mastering i.e. mistressing the world
takes fifty years to learn, is worthless

Hardwill says, you can't go backwards
or you'll have no power to—
see things as worthless. Go forward
into dungheap rationally

# CROWDED INTO A BREATHLESS BUBBLE
# OF BAD THINKING OUR POEM THE WORLD
# OWNED BY A FEW

drive towards that mountain of death in Your big bright car.
It looks like a sleek turd or onyx-jet coal
at twilight, across the desert, in Arizona, never coming
closer. No it's closer.

Go ahead and say something true
before the big turd eats You
You can say any last thing in Your poem.

———————————————

One drinks a little wine and falls asleep.
That's what bistros are for if one is a woman.
 That is,
wearing my big black winter coat I order
a *quart,* a glass and a half, of red wine.
The next thing I know, I'm waking up
having slept all night at this table
and the bistro is still open,
full of women like me in black coats, waking up.
I leave upset, anxious to get home;
later realize I haven't paid

but they'll let you sleep all night without paying

so kind the owner

while one's life's getting to be over.

———————————————

There are recurrent tableaux in a life
as ex-soldiers are haunted by battlefields.

I have one, an old apartment
dominated by a dirty black stove
crusty with grease and roach shit.

---

Young man. dark. African- or Arabic-French. friendly
has already drunk a Sunday morning drink
which I can smell, beer maybe
wears Walkman, and a fatigue jacket
I'm about twenty-five years older
in baby blue jeans, dirty Reeboks
blue sweatjacket flecks of white paint on it.
This is my everyday outfit. I'm like him. He wants to chat

He asks if I have a job. I tell him
I'm a writer and work at home
I ask him what he does, he says
he's unemployed at the moment
We're sort of the same thing. Nothing?
Some kind of liar?
On one's own.

---

Thinking of everyone whose lives . . .
and having . . .
what's there to respect? I mean I can't
respect You for anything You have
even Your job. So
who are You?

---

On Sunday night, about a block away
a homeless man was immolated

doused with gasoline, set afire and killed
by a still unknown group of four.

---

Hardwood speaking:

I think you must see that the winds of change are not
Fortune. They're the breath of the rich.
How large is human breath? Puny
but large enough to be a puny planet's misery.
The breath of a handful's a hurricane here—
a poet's breath's nothing against a rich man's breath—

Now I the Soul speak:

In the future internation
where we cry for our lost ethnicities
in this new international world,
Your poetry . . . is what?

———————————————————

I'm still frightened by the black coat bistro wine dream
I haven't remembered a dream since then
scattered, skittish
can't get down into
shelter or bring it up to surface
I want to take off that coat

yet by virtue of my education
I'm of the top tiny percent of my culture
who directs, who changes
by most standards I'm culpable, as is anyone
reading this, listening to this, here

vision of people descending a staircase
"You descend it, you dismantle it, you hurry it.
Come down, come down."
come down from that top tiny . . .

# COMING DOWN THE SPIRAL ALMANAC STAIRCASE

flowers where the *sans-abri* was killed
in front of the Church of St. Vincent de Paul
near the green fences of the street works—
huge bouquets and candles, a vigil
several people standing there

scolding signs as well: ". . . these flowers are fine but
why didn't you lend a hand? Signed
*les Miserables de 1996.*"

———————————————

A black cabbie asked
if he prefers the inaugural poem
of Robert white-as-Frost or
Maya Angelou, says,
"I'm tossed back and forth between
the two, Nuncle." Exactly

I'm the court jester if they are the court

or I'm a tennis ball
the subject of only two
possibilities.

———————————————

Both male and female but also the sign of infinity
feeding the two constantly into a central point:
that is, a bow. I walk on bow-like
message receptors of rubber embedded in the soles
of my shoes. In that oldest of puns, in the souls
        of my shoes.
One walks on, sits on, holy parts
of the body, and the lovely ambidextrous apelike hands
help me brachiate my way back to a newer

            earlier creation.
The brain isn't wires—or ability—

Define the brain    Says the Hardmitch voice

Oh
its
walls have collapsed . . .

it
spreads.

———————————————

Am I painting my white room black.
I dream that I am.
It looks kind of awful.

I know I have to go through with it.

———————————————

Mr. Subliminal Man
selling cotton candy says
he's afraid to go to Turkey because it's so dangerous.
"Oh yes," I say, ". . . Texas . . . Turkey . . . they're the same thing."
They're adjacent on the map: both on the Gulf. We're in Texas
*Turkey's so dangerous, so dangerous*
spreads out subliminally from his refreshment stand

Meanwhile or next
I'm looking at the parrot
perched over the fridge, as I'm on the phone
promising to come over, visit
The Boring Dominating One
this time a woman—in an hour, I say.
What do you do with
a woman in four-inch platforms and whore dress
who talks all the time?
If there were no sexism she
could run for the Senate

In the next dream, there was going to be
a poetry reading series
which paired a poet with an animal
for each event.

---

I'm leaving that dusty apartment again
that big dirty warehouse: no one
will help me pack. They play with the dust
or go away till I've
done it—
packed the boxes again
the same old boxes.

---

There will be no ". . . in life . . . in dream . . ."
there will be no past present and future
Texas or Turkey.
                    I will read to all the
rooms, the dark rooms,

read my poem to the long-dead as well as the future

wearing a black dress.

---

People kill each other
not because they're animals
but because they're demons.
This is obvious . . . keep
talking, anyway.
Talking to You. Is language demonic.
Obviously does
lead *You* astray.

An ape, perhaps me, perhaps an ape,
sits patiently on a bench
at the Préfecture at Cité
waiting to be admitted to France.

Can't talk here probably, can't speak French
Isn't this or that, is
a third thing

# COULD I EVER SHARE A TABLEAU WITH
# MISS JANUARY'S MURDERERS?

a succession of months in review in terms of
front-page photos on a tabloid.
The year started off really badly
January, a brunette lies bleeding and dying
her arteries having been systematically
symmetrically cut:
blood gushes from both arms
inside the elbows, for example; a pool of blood's
at her crotch.
                    Now I'm at the very event
and police are arresting the murderers.
One of the men says remorsefully,
"She wouldn't stop crying out."

        Back reading the tabloid account—
can't bear to think of anyone dying so starkly,
so uncomforted; hurry to forget it . . . Hurry on
I suppose she's me. But it's a fable of—

Stop don't always try to say. Leave it resistant
and scary, exact.

-----------------------------

My dreams have been terrifying
for two nights running.

I could just go to the movies
Indulge in everyone's violent fantasies . . .

You seem to want everyone dissected onscreen
Like a serial killer want to make sure
there's nothing there but blood,
fear, then blood.

If, then

if the disenfranchised are always doing cultural work
in the culture's unconscious
if that's what they've been doing for centuries
then . . .

because the people who have things can't do it;
and their dream, the New Yorker story, is dull.

But the *literal* dreams of the "people"
are rich with their loss and desperation; sharp feeling:
cultural richness . . .

Possibly, Mitch has just said this. He adds,

As an actor I know where the stories come from:
the air; the street. Not from Your own (owned) observation
of the trashier muter elements
but from their emotion getting under Your skin
transformed into Your exquisite fear of them.

---

I don't want out of this poem,
the way I often Want Out. After a time.
Though I've started to daydream
about having a "style." Copout.

---

Dream the desert landscape around Needles
is covered with houses which are shutters or slits
in the hills and on the level ground.
Eyes burying themselves alive. I'm disgusted . . .

---

Deep inside each cultural tableau,
a base exchange of feeling
and thinking. What's the point?
What would there be if there weren't that?

I don't know. I still don't like it
even without all this righteous or fearful
garbage we bring to every situation
doing things with others seems a pointless
sort of existence. I just don't get the point.
Figuring out how to get along every single time.

———————————————————

With my Sister Life and a man named Care
trying to get a connecting flight on Finnair.
Wind up somehow in a fabric shop
with a huge swatch of technicolor green velvety cloth
I find a ruler to measure with with a needle-like eye on top of it
Two other women working at cloth demand my ruler-needle of me
I refuse them both; one, un-
ethically, summons a man
who comes flying over the landscape
in a 19th century frockcoat and beard—
his name means More of Same—
flying by parachute, holding on to a swath
of technicolor red velvet unmeasured cloth

He's gonna steal my ruler! He's gonna change Go to Stop!
He's gonna steal my ruler and make some more of the same old shit!
He's gonna say that his is progressive and mine isn't!
He's gonna say that it's his ruler!

———————————————————

If I'm a spy here for another plane of reality
I don't really know what intelligence they want
why would anyone want to know our stuff?

———————————————————

In conjunction with a memory of Phoenix,
that desert landscape:
the pangs of a single child, myself?

the pangs of one person mean . . .

Whose experience of the world is the most important?

"Compensation for Chief Executives of Big U.S. Firms Soared 15%" in 1995.

Whose experience of the world is most important

## ECHOES THE PAST FUCKS ME OVER AND OVER

does the Past know the Future?
This dark woman says, Yes, in this game,
Yes. Her child back then
in this game of going back
knows that his father's dead now in the future
I greet him in his buggy. Wearing glasses. Intellectual baby

saying Yes, I knew all along I was born
for a future fucked up by others. But I'm smart a
human the species which wears glasses.

———————————————

Come down on ladder dream
come down
from the top of the building dream

have climbed up twice to the top at night
counting to a hundred: we're on top of the skyline, Chicago or Paris
myself and a couple of men writing; but I have fear of heights
and say, I'm sorry, I can't stay. I'm climbing back down.

So I climb back down the ladder, counting to a hundred
and then watch all the others now climbing down too
there were actually a lot, up there, above everyone.
An announcer's voice says, "In Mercedes McCambridge green . . .

Mercedes McCambridge!"
She has climbed down too.

———————————————

The Mohaves believe that all knowledge
is dreamed not learned. Or they did
believe that. A Mohave has to dream
        for her or him self
everything that Mohaves have always known.

How I am, what I know—it feels like it, mostly,
came to me in a dream

Except for what I know about war

To change the world, as I always say,
change the forms in our dreams.

_____

I'm still on top of a building
another dream says so

the umpteenth the top
floor of a Columbia dorm . . .

then I can't get my top
I mean blouse on just can't

nor can the other women
from my college year, we'll never get
to be where the men are on top

I don't even approve of the top

so how can I get permanently down
and still be equal to the men?

_____

It's a book cover encrusted with jewelry inside (again)
no pages.
It's a collage inside of jewels, in no
chronological order. Though the
jewels are knobby when it's open
they flatten when it's closed.
It has to be fastened closed, like a diary.

Perhaps tableaux over time become this encrusted jewel affair
the single dense tableau.

Dream for half a sec, that a woman making toast says brightly,
"There are only certain things that can happen!"
Another person doing something else says, "Beetles . . ."

Oh I suppose that's true, there are
only certain things that can happen.
Are the things that can't, things?
Or are we referring here
to the things that can't happen to one
due to choice, circumstance
(class, sex, race, nationality, age—)
everything in a life that's led to *this* moment

this here beetle can happen
one of these two or three beetles
glossy and sluggish.

That person that signifies me
has gotten larger. She's wearing Hardword's trenchcoat
and walks with a formidable dog.
She's worried about who's crying
in the big street-level world room.
Today, an undistinguished-looking young blonde is crying

not Whitney Houston
who perhaps should get a retroactive award
for her work in *The Bodyguard*
because it's meant more to more people worldwide
than this year's Pulitzer Prize–winning volume of poems.

Houston doesn't need another award;
neither does the Pulitzer Prize winner.
I don't   need an award   either.

This is getting to be, finally,
the poem I've always been working on . . .
but can I serve it to everyone, plate of dates?

A drift or myth in all my life's days
a what I've lived according to . . .

the idea makes me nauseous.

Down here by the rock walls outside the caves
something orange, not a flower but a colored idea of one,
floats with me. I
walk under a rock arch
sit down in a blue shadow

time-chunks hanging around here
you're a time-chunk, a real boring rock
someone can analyze:
part gneiss part petrified been-done.
Nothing that's going to happen is of any interest

## IN ANY MOVIE WHATSOEVER, IN ORDER
## TO BE WORKING ACTORS

look where it's leaking leaking from upstairs
down the walls through the storage room full of toys
because
the washing machine is on. Come down and see
how there's leaking.

———————————————————

The non-authorial possibly lyrical not-necessarily intelligible
but certainly impersonal revolutionary no-longer-an-I
has a closetful of stuff.
I don't mean "cultural baggage"
I mean literal material possessions
that Cost Money.

———————————————————

Watch the commercial for the new toy movie
the darling doughy things are in danger
it's the latest in animation
well something should be animated
but these are like pieces of molded shit
exclaiming, having adventures

I think that that movie's English
tonight's American programs are psychotic
extra-terrestrials leave their green blood
on FBI agents and Russian clones
one agent's sister's been brought up by an E.T.

another show's symbol's a blue rose
for a syndicate of assassins
which works unofficially with the President
I'm to sympathize with a rogue assassin
after his latest seven murders

and in the case of both shows believe in vast conspiracies
there are so few vast conspiracies
the rise of the multinational empires
has happened before our eyes with our consent.

———————————————

Jean-Paul Belmondo is pissed off. His new movie
is being released in comparatively few French theaters;
Disney's *Toy Story* is being released in 500 theaters across France.

———————————————

If I want to change this dream, what should I do.
I can't get hold of things with my hands
move my feet or get my blouse on—

> new kind of virtual reality game, I guess "game"
> from the Japanese, called Build Your Own Princess,
> boy builds his own dream girl—Have you heard?

That isn't a dream though.
                        This is:
a venerable prick, a sharp-tongued
poet has given a learned talk
comparing Peru and the southern United States

how fucking useful. Should I wear a mantilla
should I wear a mantilla
to the after-the-lecture party at his house?

———————————————

". . . more avant-garde than thou . . ."
That's Mitch back, making me giggle,
" 'cause only the will can be more blank than blank."

"There is no," I start automatically, "well there *is,*
I suppose, more avant-garde than thou.
But it doesn't matter. These categories
are our toys. Words like
reactionary, forward-looking, sodden leaked on
mess now . . ."

Really
can I really only be speaking
to a tiny poetry-reading
presumably mostly middle
class of people, unless I'm a movie,
can I?

The movies are probably still better than most poetry
bad as they are;
they're just so fascistically overpowering to the senses. un-
gentle. And all
for money.
An immoral art form.

---

Down in my caves:

Am
self. Overwhelmingly
the
Forbidden Self.

Message: NANCY WAS A NASTY MAN

Nancy, Nancy Reagan?

another piece of screen.

---

I felt really bad, about two days ago
that I didn't seem to be writing High Art
I was reading an essay on High Art
with excerpts from the High Artist's poems—
I thought, I could be doing that; I mean, I do Know How,
have done. But this *is* High Art . . .
Unfortunately it's fun.

Still ill; my brains are soft mucus
leaking.

Sudden tumult in caves full of black-cloaked figures
"We want your change, now"    "But I'm sick"
They want coin of roses, no the nickel I once made
out of Styrofoam and acrylic paint
All I have? I think not, and
why should they want that? they don't
They groan campily, as in *Night of the Living Dead*,
What we want what we want is you

# DO YOU WANT TO BE EXCELLENT AN A ACTRESS NO NOT THAT EITHER

the jewels speak, the different-colored
stones on a string—if I
weigh them they speak. They're
a poem I guess; but they say
who the murderers are, as well.
The murderers pull guns on "us":
so what's the point of the jewels? I mean
if the murderers just shoot us because
we know who they are

They are long-haired blonde trash
out of the movies.
                Oh.

---

The board the cave wall's
got a message on it:

I HATE NOW ART. IT STINKS OF PROGRESS.

"Who is 'I' please?" I ask the cave air.

Sound of wind. Real wind.

---

I am an orthodox religion
in a big black coat, with pockets, at night
what would be the point of all my qualities
if a certain 'you' died
oh there might be a point again
after all the suffering

I am about to be
a lesbian, in another dream
the meaning of that? it's meaningless
a great black night, don't You see, I wander lost
amid hotels and markets, stalls which sell dead things;
if you're young it's glamorous, sci-fi—if old, not.

———————————

Story is
one way to interpret experience.
What's really happening? Not
story. Not
participles. Not sentences
made from unexpected parts.
What

There's the cave door
something like
caves really happening? Tableaux?
Oh I
don't know.

———————————

It's Anne Francis, the B actress, tending bar
with her blonde hair dyed brunette.
Did she once play the female detective Honey West?
She was certainly in *Bad Day at Black Rock*.
I think, she isn't attractive but
must be photogenic—her
face is bumpy, somewhat neanderthal. Yet
protuberances of forehead, jaw, flatten on camera—
story-like: awkwardnesses disappear
she comes to fit the description, the camera.

———————————

What is this cave? Ask it.

"Old," it says, "But old is numbers.
Nothing else."

Hardwill says: "When we
are working actors, we are participating
in society, at that moment,
so are non-transcendent. This is good."

"Why? How?" the soul says, "I don't think so."

I'm the soul today. The soul is right.
I'm in a non-economic moment.

If no one knows more than I do.
Not even a *group* of You . . .

toilets, and leaking, streams of water
from above, all night
onto apartment's
stained carpet and pretense of history . . .

all pretenses seem to dissolve in the caves
though they often reappear again, lower, in dreams
out of time and washed about.
*Who's* pretentious? Anyone
enters pretense an emotion, the excitement
of believing what she or he says.
Building a new house
another one. Wow. I mean
she's telling a new kind of story. It's so
hallucinatory. apocalyptic. What progress.

Society is
a huge
cohesive
emotion.

I can extract myself
from that emotion

for moments.

---

Going to give poetry reading, I'm supposed to be late
in long blue lowcut 50s evening dress
Marilyn Monroe comes to get me at nine—I'm
late enough but won't be as late as *she* used to be.
She's wistful about my success
helps me with my neckline, fixes its lace of wire rings
so only one ring dangles down "undone . . ."

Absolutely inside The Emotion.

---

Not sure whether one attempts life outside it (The Emotion)
becomes involved in changing it, or both variously

don't want to
live inside it, must etc, sticky love
and animal obligation?
many animals are ghosts now

# WE SHOULD ALL LIVE LIKE ROCKS IN A FLAT FIELD

in the caves today
the pistil of a calla lily may be speaking:

. . . THE ROOF IS FALLING

The caves are membranes breathing, huge
petals the sun breaks through
soft skin greenhouse.

Must I experience total
collapse of psychic hierarchy?
Will the caves stop being caves?

Leveling. Everything's leveling.

———————————————

Self-important? What's really that
is this
outmoded trivial talk of revolution
the poet's wistful desire
to shed a lot of blood. Disgusting,
and irrelevant now.

———————————————

Memory of dream of rock star blends with memory of newscast,
Liberian children with rifles
"Boys make good soldiers": their commandant
"If I tell them to cut out the eyes, they do"
But a boy interviewed apart from him says,
"If I don't do what he tells me to he'll kill me."
What country did they buy those
guns from? U.S.? England? Russia? Maybe France—Iran—Israel . . .

My friends from high school
carry handguns now. I mean the women

according to a
friend, a couple of them
brought their guns to our thirtieth
class reunion.

---

It all topples when I'm alone and bored
Conclusion?
To promulgate "revolution" everyone
should spend more time alone
and bored.

---

Your eyes, when they haven't been cut out
cannot be
"read"
they are Yours
anyway the "print paradigm is outmoded" I'm told.

The Liberian boy, being a boy, is hoping for a future.

The people who discuss

are proud participants

to be alive in exciting times

transition for boy a computer

we can give him in the year 2010 or a job in

a glass eye factory—

future glass eyes that can see
that can watch television—
eyes perfected by
Viacom or MGM.

Sudden wave of, feeling what
was it, almost scent of
being high on Something 25, 26 years ago—
speed maybe. That was great
useless, destructive, irrelevant, demonic
What's different from that? Anywhere?
No,
          no
I won't ever do it again.
I'm supposed to help make all the other
people, near and far and very far, in the
whole world, happy. Oh I will. Because
everyone's so deserving.

I can barely see Mitch's face anymore
I'm suffering loss of character

I lost Soulgirl, as character, a long time ago
simply became her.

"Have you met the *psych et po* feminists?
You sound just like them."

I'm on my own, bored, obnoxious
out of touch with the premier print paradigm people
of my time.
              This must be Paradise, Paris
not Liberia.

    SONG

    Clear enough
    Clear enough
    Who ever
    Wanted to be anywhere
    But here but . . .

Clear enough
Clear enough
Who ever
Wanted to be anywhere
But here but . . .
                    (repeat endlessly)

# EVERYONE'S OUT AFTER SOME EMOTIONAL ACTION

where are we in this dark copse
thank god I got here, shadows
on Mitch-ham's face: "the process
of leveling is proceeding too erratically"

"Can't concentrate, must change," I say, sigh
because I hate to be so deliberate.

———————————————

Dreamed of a poetry institution
several rooms, resembling a bank, windows with grilles.
There are no bathrooms. If you must shit
do it at the threshhold between rooms a veil descends

to cover you during the act and then
the extrusion itself seems magically to disappear.
I shit at a couple of threshholds but
finally get to leave, skip out
of the building. Sunshine outside, for a change.

———————————————

All the times I've been "bad."
Am I interested? No I'm

not interested. Hurt people's feelings?

A suspect category of happenstance.

———————————————

A group of ten or so "liberals"
rob a bank to publicize their cause.
As a result, a woman I know well
is now both lacking an arm and dead.
She and I stand discussing this

near a steep drop in the landscape.
I may be dead too; but I am not a "liberal . . ."

In the next dream I will slide down a cliff, slide down
At the bottom, of the dam—
a dam not a cliff's now suggested—would be
that white-foamed emerald water
I've always been terrified of
It's what's at the bottom of Hoover Dam

I guess I have to slide down
that damned conservative dam
and join the scary water, I'll get washed through
we're the river. Nothing but the river.
Non-political.

_____

. . . Sluggish going to the door
for the mail.
So the mailman drove a bulldozer through
the front of the house: the mail
was deposited by dirteater maw onto the floor.
The news had arrived.

_____

. . . I go about
just detached from The Emotion—am not
in Your story. When I remember. It's a physical
sense of detachment—a sac no
longer adhering to a flesh wall.
Having been ripped away.

_____

Leaving people at a cafe, I can cross the river
to my other room—of course I have two—
and change my clothes. My room over here is a dark one

when I open my jewelry boxes
voices talk referring to me in the third person, saying things like
"We're Alice's jewels. She's with us now"

But the earrings I want aren't in this room
they're back in the other one, though I see
some edible earrings and also amethysts and emeralds.

———————————————

Having trouble feeling involved with
the news. Same old Men. Same old
no one to say to them, Piss Off I'm
tired of the spotlit-figure form of govt.

———————————————

So at this large hotel, towards 8 o'clock in the
morning, night had become day.
There was a lake outside, lots of people
they said they wanted to see the monster
something like the Loch Ness monster
sightings have been reported, in that very lake.

Then I saw it.
        A skatelike fish

though not flat, the size of a whale

pale delicately modeled tumbling absolutely lovely . . .

People said There it is, but not excitedly, and then left

One woman selling beads to the tourists said to me, You were
       so lucky to have seen it.

But hadn't she seen it? Not really.

It didn't seem to make an impression on anyone but me

I've awakened knowing I've seen it, seen "it" in "life"

# SEEN THE WHALE-SKATE AND SEEN A TOMB

watching the terrible movie *Nixon* last night,
from scene of young Dick driving past
20's postcard palms in orange light, L.A. sky,
reminded of how we in Needles called L.A. "Inside":
"He moved somewhere Inside." Everyone
said and says it, usage particular to a
desert town which is very much Outside.

———————————————

I milled about in an opera audience all night
the opera was never happening,
only the audience was.
At one point I found a group
of nude women in black thighhighs

who I thought were performing the opera
they were just rehearsing bits
of popular favorites: "Fire Dance," "Sextet" from *Lucia*.
I returned into the audience
way way up in the balcony, the cheap seats I guess.

Can everyone who ever lived be here?

———————————————

Rain all day, Pentecost
no fire on head.

Stood in Louvre line 20 minutes
would have to stand
another hour, gave up—

I have a feeling I'll never go in again.
Never not like that anymore.
Similar to the traffic, and pollution.

———————————————

"Most people's minds are vile . . ."
read that or similar in sci-fi novel
by Octavia E. Butler, yesterday, leads me
to ponder what my mind would be like
if a telepath's mind invaded it . . .
Should I have a better, prettier, sweeter,
calmer, nobler, mind? It's similar to
the god-knows-your-every-thought
kind of idea. Then, there's no reasoning left,
though the world becomes *good*. I think.
I was once *good* for several weeks
rather recently, but I could only posit
one writing style from that
and seemed to have less and less to say.
I *was* happy.

---

Dream a huge bandage of adhesive tape
is placed on my front torso; will hurt like hell when removed.
The area of concern is my navel . . . Why?
It sort of has to be held in for a while—
I have to be more tightly wrapped? Why?

Fête des Papillons, on rue Papillon
with cages of . . . live papillons!

Got warm. It finally got warm yesterday.

---

. . . in contact with some new
part of me. In the dream story of myself
over which I have no control
not the partially willed caves-&-Mitch-ham narrative.

In this dream, having gone low I must go lower
the method of descent involves scrunching oneself
into a place, in between two places,
which doesn't appear to be there.
I find such a place in an underpass—
leprous people in rags; dark papers, filth
scattered. A dirty

man shows me the spot and says, "You will meditate
in a room which contains a tomb."

Now, in the room, it's too dark at first
then light, there's the mound of the tomb with its
plaque—I'm scared. Room's too small.
No the room opens out
into a hall where a knight stands with his family
but they aren't human. Their faces
are made out of leather, with metal-studded seams, glass eyes.
The man wears the usual Knights Templar outfit.

_____

I wonder what's
written on the tomb.

_____

Submitted to the nice
though capricious-seeming ministrations
of someone I don't like, all night.
We may both be ill; I stoically
accept her though don't need
her or her care. It seems.
Maybe the real illness is that self-
satisfying niceness
she's exhibiting, and my stoicism;
or perhaps I do have to let others
slobber all over me.
(Do I?) To go lower; also to level. I hope not.

_____

I'm meditating near the tomb
wearing the knight's costume

Just sitting on the ground, leaning against the wall
in the dark—there's a little light but
can't read the plaque on the tomb.
Is the plaque empty

I'll have to drag all this shit up to the surface soon

# KEEP GOING DOWN TO THE TOMB

my tee-shirt is inside out
so I can't see the words I'm
wearing. They're backwards
next to my chest.
This is being casually dressed,
is a possible fashion, and also odd.

———————————————

Now it's nearly summer,
most of a year gone since I began this poem.

In the Alpine Garden at the Jardin des Plantes
blue things are back, dark blue on stalks.
Despite pollution that's
visible, breathable everywhere. Period.
Nobody *really* cares.
We're selfish and stupid. Still.

———————————————

This asshole prof. crit.
asserts that a certain novel
by his otherwise hallowed subject is flawed
because it features the minds and vocab
of "two unintelligent women"
just some vapid showgirls.

                           Nobody knows who
lives in this world.
At any rate, no one "intelligent" seems to know.

———————————————

I forget why she said that
I didn't belong there. The real
reason is that she doesn't

like my poems.
I sort of like the fact that she dislikes them
that she's so programmed
I've enjoyed being scornful, in my life

                                     When I was

young, a child and perfect, I didn't
but that was before I knew how wide-
spread sexism is, even
among my sex. This woman thinks I'm
courtesy of my first husband.
That's my just name . . . that's
my career.
                One purpose of heights
is to be scornful from them,
so I will probably still maintain some.
Scorn as a value.

---

A door of the caves opens out
onto level ground today
the landscape out there's partly cloud-covered
dark sky over far hills—Arizona.

But I want to be near the tomb and so wish myself down.

I'm the knight again, in mail and red cloth,
nothing happens. Mitch, Hardknight, nothing's happening
because I have my period and can't think.

You don't have to think, he says

The tomb's like a hawk, a mask, I say, No it's stupid a cliché

Not stupid, he says, If you will die.
Is everyone who ever lived *here?* Yes.

---

Someone has come to fix the plumbing.
About time . . .

in the living room's a whole young
punkish culture, well, really
bleachhaired kids dressed in black body-pierced
their folkways
probably won't make it out of this living room
won't last past their 30th year
so talk to them now; it's fun
Hi, kids.

---

We're letting him be an alcoholic
it's not as bad as letting everyone
drive their silly-fuck cars.
Anyway he's dead; we already did it
the doorbell rings, I answer it
It's the plumber again
he wants to finish the job and we've
already paid him.
But I thought it was supposed to leak . . .
until there was an absolute flood and the whole
structure collapsed . . . His name is Jim.
Isn't everyone's. I really don't
want him to fix my plumbing.

---

Being scornful I seem to begrudge
X her moment of pure self
It's okay she still has it. Unless I kill her, maybe . . .
she actually begrudges me mine all the time
denying the existence of a pure self. That's
what the Oppressors do . . .
what they've always done. Though Xtians
say the pure self's there after you've done what they say
taken a bath to their prescription.
Actually the Illuminati of every discipline
are careful to say You must do as I do
to be yourself. And don't be irritable

Hand holds reddish grail cup
reddish trim, glass—
scrollwork delicate but commonplace in conception
well made beachware-type ware.

Everyone's coughing this week
pollution or pollen? Who knows

Who I am is worn inside
not social like words on a shirt
. . . Is that good or bad or *is*
Obviously, *is*

no plaque on the tomb
no words on the shirt

## NOT THAT PERSON ANYMORE,
## MITCH BEING EVER FAINTER

can't get to the island reserved for me
the rich hold me back
I have to make the rich a cup of tea
they've shown up unexpectedly this
morning; so, out buying tea for the rich
I pee all over myself, under
my housecoat, walking down the street.
The pee evaporates quickly after all;
if I can just get the rich out of my
house I'll go off to the island.
My lover's rented it for me to be alone on,
for a day and a half.

———————————————

All that stuff about E's was because
all that stuff about E's
was because I kept seeing E's graven
        on the cave walls
a most common letter?
E is for pee, the flood of commonality
produced by tea, commonality
The rich *always* have to have some of everyone's.

———————————————

Fell into a despair
yesterday afternoon
the moment I was coming down
with a light cold
grieving, grieving for what, grieving for the future.

An American West of colored plates
in a library, library books:
watercolor-pale sagebrush
and paloverde trees, is a dream. Is it over?

Pick up that cherry pit. Throw
it away, it's sterile.

---

I saw him, what a jerk
well he was acting friendly
I ran past his car; felt guilty, a little
but I had to keep on running
stay faster than he was in order to stay so
fast, to be just this fast. He
always pretends to be nice, but he's
dominating as hell. Everyone, for some
reason, says, "What a nice man!"
I ran right past him, forever?
Is no such thing, I suppose, no such thing
as hardly anything we do. All the best craftsmen,
oh yes he's one of them . . . I'm better, but what's that—
a full grail? What's that? He thinks he knows
what poetry is: what he and his friends write.

---

Dead roses from Neuilly.

I crawled into the tumulus, that tomb,
to see what was in there. Now *I'm*
in here. I
knew that—

the Will is dead here. I mean Mitch
is sort of dead.

---

The grail's full of pee which
smells like herbs.

---

A tall building in Barbés
an apartment on the top floor, un-
remarkable, large; I visit it casually
prepare to leave but
the owner wants me killed for having seen it

                his "man" chases me
I make it to elevator
door shuts, descent, struggle of buttons
as I'm halfway down, with his "up" button
he tries to pull me back up but
I press my "down" button hard, hold it
I win. I escape temporarily
I think, what a tacky movie!

later that night, on the Bowery, in a 40's
movie with The Bowery Boys
I've been accepted as dark
in the bodega, they said I was
dark enough to hang out on the stoop
I'm young and beautiful, denim skirt, jewelry.
The man called The Snowman
gets out of his car and says repeatedly to me,
"I'm gonna shape you up!"
I laugh; I don't have to do anything but be a poet.

———————————————

Heads of state, males dressed like sheikhs
kiss each other on the lips
they're really vying to perform a favor
for an international celebrity—another man
an athlete or singer—

in a large empty room with a microphone—
they're pecking, pecking.

———————————————

. . . a radiant
paloverde tree
a heavenly tree in
my mother's backyard:
a dream.

———————————————

Enter earth through narrow cave as at Sisteron
walking through corridor, behind others

holding candlelights, haloes.
Then room dark, people asleep on the ground
in a rose formation, bodies curved petals.
And there's nothing else here, right now
all my mysteries are up there in
the fragile upper air.

---

Once more evinced
a cruder personality
to talk to someone who's difficult
for me.

World of half-light

Don't really have to take care of myself

I've come down to the ground floor; now
I'm going up to it

# FOUR SCARVES AND A LION

---

*(JUNE 18, 1996–AUGUST 28, 1996)*

## HAVE I BEEN HERE BEFORE IS
## SOMETHING UNFAMILIAR

in Normandie
climb down rungs of steel ladder
as if down to canyon;
walk among rocky tidepools, hurt feet
to see limpets and *bigorneaux,*
half-eaten cuttlefish, eggcase exposed;
people are collecting *bigorneaux* in sacks . . .
walk further out onto rocks
in a tableau, a long frame of time,
not a person, until leaving:
as in the caves am non-historical.

———————————————

A poet dressed as a saloon girl
red dress, black
ostrich feathers in her hair—
that's so unlike her,
she's really a grouchy intellectual

I was going to help her perform her prose poems,
in a cage, a sort of prison
maybe it was just a disco cage;
the poems were written in bamboo,
bamboo words, hard to decipher . . .

Exactly what it's like, what it's all like. Poetry world.

———————————————

Hear in my mind, *ne touches pas*
What, I ask silently
I see a grail, a glass grail rimmed
with glass roses. Who's speaking?
All of tradition.
*Let it stay just the way it is*

A question of a large package, a big cardboard envelope
entitled DISOBEDIENCE. A member of a girl group
asks me where the comic poet's things are:
DISOBEDIENCE belongs to the comic poet,
she's clear about this. It isn't the comic poet's
lectures on Thoreau, but the comic poet's
own book, DISOBEDIENCE.

What a strange and interesting woman, ugly
full of tension, glasses
in a red roses dress hating me
because my feet had been up on the métro seat
before she sat down.

This guy doesn't seem to have
actually *read* my essay. I
never mentioned "the author"—
the author as important—
as he asserts . . . was talking about
the epic, as composed of
cultural materials, including measure.

Now I'm talking about epic
as Voice. and as
disobedience. For
example I have disobeyed his chart, or is it
charter—Your, Yours, Yours.
Your idea of how I'm supposed to write.

There's conscious and un-
conscious    or there's conscious
semi-conscious (self-
hypnotized)    and the various
levels of unconsciousness: dreams, and then
below that
is that grailish?

                    To make it all
more conscious I have flooded it with
my voice    without
trying hard to make my voice sound like a poem.
A voice is more uniting than . . .
it's all we've got to do it with.
The mind by itself is fuzzy enslaved
and divided. Written words, by themselves,
are E's.

---

I try the caves again, out of habit, but
to get to them I find I'm
climbing down the rungs of the Normandie ladder

and the caves are different, with a potted geranium,
red, suspended just below a rock arch—
the caves are rooms, are stores
are like the upper world.

The general store is lined with books
a man tends bar in front of them. I order
*Outline of History*, fall asleep into the white blaze of its
pages, sitting at a table.

I sense Hardwood's face when I wake up
it's opaque and dark, with black tunnel eyes
I'm hard all over, harder than ever

# THERE WAS ALSO VALIUM IN THE DRINK, PLACED THERE BY TWO OTHER PEOPLE

you had, effectively, drugged me, but
what I saw on the drug was true
you put acid in my drink without telling me, so
I would loosen up and be fun for you
but what I saw was that the historical portraits
of fat wigged men were alive
and ranged a gamut of demonic expression.
Then I blacked out; you told me, later,
I'd said that the way my brother had died
made everything seem worthless; I'd shouted
at you that your essays on war were self-gratifying.
Oh yes, history. You said that I
should have seen his life as a speck of loss in the struggle,
immense and longterm, of an Asian nation,
a spark to balance against 20 Asian sparks—
how fucking comforting!
Perhaps you could die too, to help make enough
counter-balancing sparks? Well, who then
would write your poems, I suppose you'd say.
There was raw meat throughout the house:
I'd attacked the paintings
and only raw steak could heal them. I
can believe that. But there's always plenty of raw meat to heal
hurt power. Think of how much there is in Asia
All those people, sweatshops, markets, all that offending
new capitalism. Better organize a special issue, a panel, on the subject
your pretty house may be in danger, from capitalism . . .
(you are not a capitalist, you merely own a house.) Happy Acid Trip!

———————————————————

Have forgotten the other you . . .
that sense that some other entity knows one intimately
from the inside.

It's probably part of oneself
why shouldn't it be
why shouldn't part of one, be "god?"

Could "god" "know" a "person?"
if god is ground
god could be in a person, could be like a person

having to mimic our every idiocy.

---

The evening news is gratifying
Le Pen-is is fucking up
Le Pen-is doesn't think the French
football team is really French.
He does
look like an organ, such a wee-eyed prick of a figure
bluntheaded thicknecked bald.

---

The man I shouted at in the acid dream
had a name that meant "white fluid." My seeing to
embrace "black" then—
you might say that's racist . . .

Language tends to be racist, exists to make distinctions,
as, likewise, do images;
but there can be a personal reality which isn't devisive,
between words or frames.

The rifts in the world cannot be healed with language.

Though poetry modifies the divisiveness of words with
light and fluidity—true self,
raceless and sexless, burning through language's flaws.

---

I don't want to go down into the caves anymore.
I try to summon the 'feeling' of the caves
without a descent into their imagery . . .

The crystal I'm in's not yet as intense as previously.
Then there's imagery anyway:
A black cowl blowing and twisted
the glass grail floats precariously on
a sinister breeze, all in a black sky

We're happening millenia ago.

———————————————

In Paris a woman scowls. Eyebrows and downdroop
mouth: she's conveying her dress to work on
the rue du Faubourg-Poissonnière. She scowls straight at me.
She's not a dream. I dream of an acquaintance
in another social class, as I'd perceived that in my youth,
wears a mask in three colors to speak of her own
father's death. Black, white, rust-red
the mask shows me she's my equal
and that both his death and that equality are what's holy. I
wake up ashamed. I dream of the evaporation
of a relation's beauty. She waits for me
to push her in her wheelchair, her foot is missing
I can't tell if she's she or my sort-of enemy
No there's the sort-of enemy, they both look like someone else a
Ms. Fleeting, another woman, but an older Ms. Fleeting,
because we're all older Ms. Fleetings. Or Jo Van Fleets—she's
just died . . . So let's
serve the damned meal, in the next dream please. My mother says,
The continuousness of this dinner party
as an event that isn't divided, rigidly, into PIECES of caring
is what's so good about it. We don't have to
keep our services separate:
we DON'T have to have classes. of people, experience, culture
we DON'T HAVE TO take care of someone needy for
an hour at three. We are feeding everyone
period. We don't care about your special problems.
We're tired of thinking about who you are.
If food's all you need . . . Isn't it?

I can't undo anything; this poem

Left a house again all night, packing up

leaving that house

# I DON'T HAVE SYMPATHY WE'RE EQUALS

I'm supposed to read from
my diaries. The audience
awaits my life
I want to read my love poem by
me, François Villon, no
I mean me.
Miss Ellie from *Dallas* says that life's horrible
offstage, to no one at all
her life and she are a fiction. Mine and I
François' and he, are not:
Our emotions
terrify and transform us    Our lives
have a will of their own. That's why
people want to hear
our diaries.

———————————————

Tired of trying to seem as smart
as the ones who say We're the smart people?
They say they are so get to be
They've been to see the Wizard

So get yourself a certificate of intelligence!

I'll give you one. It's part of the meal. Why not?

> This certifies that
> (fill in name) is Wise enough to be
> in the General "Burning" Conversation.
> Just as she/he is

> > ". . . if I burn, I am saved
> > if I'm saved, I do not burn . . ."

(Signed)

Alice Notley

---

How to kill a lion: These methods
involve large canopic jars.
Specifically, different treatments
of the lion's head are proposed.
Sometimes the head's left intact; sometimes it's
crushed or shrunken

      : the *têtes de veau*
      the milkwhite heads, eyes delicately closed
      lined up on TV last night

. . . a dream about the subjugation of all wildness.

---

The "serial tweaker"
it says in this paper
doesn't kill, is content to
    pull out
the eyelashes
of his victims
one by one . . .

the man's a philosopher!

---

The veau drinks from the Grail—how—
In the red-dark in its stall—how
Do you know? But that doesn't
Justify its captivity—How

Do you know? I saw a tableau.
Who suffers more, I or a veau
A veau is unable to disobey   A veau
Suffers   drinks from the Grail   but suffers.

Driving in the mostly tame wilds of southern France.
A hand-painted sign says, "See God in 3 kilometers."
Follow the sign: arrive at 'God'
a wooden train, stuck in the earth,
all its machinery still going.
People had built a train of wood
on a track in a deep fosse they'd dug. But
they stopped digging the fosse:
the train's head's stuck, against a wall
of earth, its wheels turning . . .

An old dream. In front of
an ornate brown ivory—or was it wooden—
Gothic shrine, a nun
hands me a poem
carved into a small
slab of amethyst.
Not this poem, an earlier one—how
beautiful it was
                this poem's a stuck
wooden train

wood is wild, wild and mad, natured.

Drag the train up out of the canyon.

Juppé asking rhetorical questions, last night, guilty.
Being guilty a continuous state un-
perceived, seemingly, by the guilty, inside himself.

I was outside him, watching the show on TV.
To blame him for something isn't to get very far?
To blame You is better

This is the way up, pulling the train up, cursing in the old
way of this poem

## POURING RAIN NO LOVE FROM THE WEATHER
## EXCEPT IN MY DREAM

inside this sleeping compartment
of the train parked in desert flatland
between Searchlight and Railroad Pass,
waiting to go—I lie down; a lot
of Mohaves are getting on the train.
Soldiers too with their girlfriends.

The sun blazes outside.

———————————————

In dreams I'm not very sensed
I have the senses of the train, as god: e.g. bliss
      an intellectualized
velvet light breeze
plays my skin, sometimes

but I'm never hot or cold. I see, hear, am located
not always well or exactly
What's exact
is I, whose particulars may not be mine.
I is never another.

———————————————

Was I young and naked, or
a certain age and naked, in another
      dream?
Or both, there was nostalgia
for being young and naked—
a very young man was attracted to me and
hated himself for that

I was old and young
as I am.

I'm enjoying acting important
in a big black hat which
blocks out the sky—

but it's NYC or Paris, so
the sky's a piece of shit—

Otherwise dressed, again, in a showgirl's
brief outfit, black
with black spike heels,
waggle my
ass.

---

Wasn't using all of myself because
I was just looking, so I—screamed.

---

. . . the core of oneself
is spelled with a "k" it is "kor."

      Playing
with a toy volcano
in a house of gossip, I was my
polite, groveling persona.

Well I am a volcano with a core.

Another dream says "don't hide them too fast"
meaning this accumulation
of remarks, so culture-specific . . .

Will the Sinocentric or other
future admire this
work? it isn't
'universal' enough?—

the assed soul the poem
issues from *is*

universal enough—
my
kor

Kore emerges from under, and speaks:

> "The problem of my subsequent generations:
> poets, i.e. people, change their poems radically
> but not their lives."

>             I can't dissolve
> the lines between the sections of this poem
> except in my life.
> The lines won't all vanish until the moment I die.
> Though some of them will; some of them have.

---

. . . the most depressing city in the world
when the sun's hidden for two weeks.
Just another place where people scramble, anyway . . .
the Capital. They sell a lot of shoes here.

Villon was imprisoned at Châtelet
He was also a friend of a king—that sealed
him up in literary history.

Once he killed a priest in self-defense

One priest
is not enough, in self-defense

I didn't ASK to dream about him.

---

I dream a different way awake, still

that how I'm asked to see us is real
a pleasant-looking person is of value

the more obviously
crazed unpleasant one, filth, mouthing filth
can't be telling the truth. People who say
there is no truth, are pleasant-looking people, certainly,
jobs, dresses, admit the filth
under the aegis of the filth's truthlessness
and their own compassion.
Unfortunately the filth
sound as if they believe
in the truth and not in compassion.
There I side with the filth . . . "You want to kill me;
you're stealing my poems; god speaks through my mouth"

# ROARING BEING A GIVEN, MY ROARING'S A GIVEN

I said in the middle of the night I would
remember but I don't: only, Four scarves and a lion . . .
blue, red, white . . .

_____

Along the Normandie coast

and each cove contains stuff for me to find
*pretty* detritus, and sky-blue stuff, organic
blue slimy seaweed matter. I am proceeding
from cove to cove.
Later it's night and I'm in
a room full of books overlooking the ocean—
a close relative's there. Dead

Don't not believe the dead aren't alive or you'll drown.

The coves are caves, opened out.

_____

"If they're putting so much money into that,
why the hell aren't they backing it?" . . . poetry anthology.
Backing the un-
polluted detritus of the future dead
haunting You already.
I am haunting You, roaring.

_____

The gossip's affairs between women poets: someone
holds up the newspaper account—
One woman's new slim volume
called *Heterosexuality*
is the subject of her own snotty irony.
Well I don't care about this shit

Or the homo- or heterosexual Ages of Gold.
The Age of Gold is always a conceit
devaluing one's own minute. Forget it
gold is the color of one of the scarves,
light opening over the Manche, the lovely
Sleeve
of the omnisexual dead, everyone.

———————————————

. . . Stories of the white light.
These meek little Greek fathers
have not let any women
near the light for 1500 years. That is,
no women are permitted on the mountain—
where all the holy events
occur. So, I don't believe a word—
isn't light; isn't holy. More stories.

Tell me more stories, my friend,
of your victimization; how vividly
you are the focus of everyone's
words and looks; we've chosen you
to be our little martyr: you will still
bless us with your works, which are great
in fact the only—the *only* poems.

———————————————

It snowed, in July, in the Alps, last night
I'll have a mammograph today
Haiku.

———————————————

The lion.
As babies roar.
Light, dark, roar

and I remember that
X wouldn't let me breathe, placed
a white cloth over my face—

roar it away. Wet washcloth of
mannered cleanliness.
                    Clean feelings,
there are no clean feelings.

———————————————

I'm going to have the operation
in front of the hospital, but
it can't take place right now
I go home shoeless, I've lost them
Dogshit on the stairs from a puppy
Walk in the pale muck. Everyone's
just waking up

You have defined degradation:
Walking in shit. Well, that's not it.

On a taxi ride: my lover and I
get out and jog, with the driver, uphill.
All the way to the cemetery.
My lover goes into the crypt first—
I'll join him in 24 hours and there's
the button that opens the door
this is how I'll enter, small

You have defined degradation:
Painful death. Well that's not it.

Second Avenue, New York night
looking at shop wares, a lot of amber
A rosary of amber beads is really
a G-string or pelvic tassle,
"for exotic dancers only." Of course
I buy it. It's beautiful
I'll wear it

I have defined degradation:
Your valuing of present time
above sacred time and its site
in the world's body.

I've moved to another city . . .
It's either Chicago or Paris
I live in a house I like
it occupies its lot in the usual foursquare
manner and yet
I'm inside and outside it, at the same time
it's a transparence, a cross-section,
a coincidence of inside and out.

———————————————

Inside of holy time.
A window with a deciduous forest in it
moonlit leaves, this morning
No the moonlight's all over the Colorado River Valley—
No, it's here surrounding my body,
making me shiver.

Young then, young now.

Brushed by the black peacock's tail

# THE LINES FALL AWAY SOMETIMES

my beloved relation is caring for other people's children—
three girls and a boy
who's like her own son when he was young.
These daughters of my old enemy need a bath; the son
doesn't bathe, is afraid to; perhaps the daughters are only,
a long time ago, myself and my sisters.
There's too much noise outside:
my beloved relation will vigorously complain, taking
her car but takes too long
to return with no car, just a cane
and a new hairdo. She says,
"the Lord giveth and the Lord taketh away, Blessed be the name
        of the Lord . . ."


                    Awake
The latter quote
                I agree with in part as follows:
Disagree strongly with the word the Lord.
Agree strongly with the word Blessed;
don't agree much with the phrase, the name.
So though I don't approve of the whole phrase,
the name of the Lord, I think that in conjunction with loss
as outlined in giveth and taketh away,
Blessed be the name of the Lord
represents the only rational philosophy possible.

———————————————

Keep going to parties,
drink too much talk
too much—not
sleeping well;
and certainly can't breathe
this pollen-imbued air.

                    Love is
preferable to compassion; creates
equality.

I've missed the *Dallas* reruns all week.
*La grande bagarre pour Westar*—will
Sue Ellen take down Ji Er
before the series ends, a couple of years ago?

_____


The man I'm going to marry, one of the most
famous novelists in the world—dead—
is kissing his daughters on Christmas Eve, children from
the now dissolving marriage. I must be discreet still around them. But
suddenly in this large crowded hall like a festive
hotel lobby, I can't remember my relation to him,
except that it's one of affection,
so I kiss him too. I later say, It was as if I were in another
reincarnation; I knew I was related to you
but not how: I thought perhaps I was your daughter . . .

Interpret this feministically or cosmologically . . .
not both at once, or one will be a poet—
                                        Yes I'm
fated evilly to cycles of wife- and daughter-ism; also, yes,
I've always known you and the love is the same, erotic
or not, centrally, a love that's pure Relation . . .

His mother will make me clean spots off the banister
and wear the blue chiffon woman-dress.
This brick house the same as every other house on
        the street . . .
If the relations between the sexes
are changing, awake, these houses are not.
We change into another kind of
        Same As Each Other:
The world wants that. I can't find my house. I'm
not the same as you, in spite of the fact that I'm purely
related to everyone.

Bernard Tapie has to go to jail.
He's having a new set of diva emotions—
resignation, plus the urge to confess
      Last night's
aria the best

                  He should
go to jail in a red brick house
in a factory town, in my dream
          somewhere on
the outer curve of Christmas—the birth of
the beloved male,
                Oh, Yuck.

Men still don't want
to find out what women know
are unwilling to change the nature of
political dialogue

in government rooms or domestic rooms
or even on poetry panels

to accommodate how
women know.

The emotional tone of our politics
will never change

Humanity *will* disappear

My dreams are deepening, lengthening, battering
me; I have also walked
the most luxuriant of lawns

and searched for dropped valuables
in the grass—nothing there except bliss

the others left and didn't leave a thing

# THE SUBTERRANEAN SENSES ARE ALREADY THERE
# IN NEW AIR

oh countenance the upstairs harmonica player

She's a middle-aged French woman
now dolefully playing
"America the Beautiful."

———————————————

"I can't find . . . the voice won't go there . . .
where the thumb-sized Self
grows into the only flower, allthing."

Go back to school as me old     (Barnard)
Have left a class to find a bathroom
Run into man who's my ride, who wants to take me home *now*
Because *he* has the day off. Talking about getting home
I miss the whole class. Trudge with my sister past towers.

———————————————

I experience "liberation" in a dream . . .
I'm liberated from the Marché Saint-Quentin—
        obviously San Quentin Prison—
the covered market of meat and vegetable stalls
on the corner of Blvd. Magenta and rue de Chabrol.
There's a sense that some men inside
are evil to prevent liberation—I ride
on the shoulders of my friend, a tall black man—
"We'll get you your Lib- er- a- tion," he says

and carries me, with a bodyguard along, up some stairs
to the liberating machine, a globe-like sculpture
with spaces between the "continents"; standing inside
the sculpture, I'll escape through the spaces
I whoosh upwards; awaken with an
overwhelming rushing sensation

fall back asleep into a story of defecting to Russia;
but Moscow is, temporarily, Peoria, California: and I
must rescue a bludgeoned Spanish man—"I practice
Spanish War," he says. Another man has just
said, "I practice French war."

---

. . . world dissolution
of national borders through computers . . .
conquered, everyone conquered—
'not since the Romans'

In the years when deregulation was achieved,
aided by deregulation of literature,
which dissolved into a conversation about writing,
all opinions competing equally . . .

that was about jobs.
Everyone just wanted a job. The structures of power
were frozen, inside all that machine mobility.
Everyone sucked ass.

---

". . . a clocharde like me," the woman said, laughing;
why not. I like her better than

But I'm too lazy to be anything; I just write

just a shade, just a shade lazier, I might really whoosh.

---

The lines aren't really disappearing

Well then maybe they don't have to

Don't confuse theory and living form . . .

I think I've glimpsed the liberation dress
in the shortest of dreams:
an archaic pattern or design, without a ground,
contoured as if to fit an invisible person:

there's a pattern for the headpiece and a pattern for
the body. The ground of the pattern is spirit.

———————————————

Meeting a woman in the bleachers
on the Columbia University Campus
between Butler and Lowe Libraries:
we will pose nude
to publicize our cause. A somewhat
retarded woman with whom I went to school in Needles
has left a note stating she
wants to pose too.

———————————————

Someone's—is it my skin
is covered with lesions:
as the doctor cures them she dies.
Are they the liberation pattern falling off? . . .
The cure killed her . . . Is she now dead,
as in society's thing, or dead and reborn?

I refuse to die like that!

The young biker woman smashes her bottle
on the sidewalk of Avenue Tolbiac; green glass everywhere
now she can stop being angry
at her boyfriend; she and he leave.

A man from McDonald's comes out and sweeps up the glass.

———————————————

Can you see that something inside
keeps calling one home
through dreams

# REMEMBER THE STATION WITH NO NAME

five francs yesterday
to an aggressive-looking young French man
with glazed eyes and facial contusions

Ten francs recently
to a grey-haired American woman
who said she anticipated a changed
situation and various jargons

Five francs recently to an
African man with a rip in his pants
along the seam of the waist,
pissed off.

———————————

When the métro stops this time, there's
no name in the station; instead
of a name a silver glittery
cloud of paint on the wall.

At the station with no name
righteousness dissolves.

My responsibility: less
to others than to the station it-
self. I know

that doesn't sound right to you;
I think it's true.

———————————

Go into a bisexual bathroom where I
must undress and bathe before several men.
Patrick Poivre D'Arvor, the newscaster,
is seated on a toilet, inside a stall;

two other men are around.
I undress coolly though my abdomen protrudes.
One man says to me sympathetically,
"It's like when I had a note from Prince Sihanouk
pinned to my back, that fame . . . "
New York night's just there, towards a cafe, Veselka's.

In another dream, famous rock star's here at our party.
I'm in my own conversation. Finally
he asks me a question and so
I overtly recognize him; the minute I do
he withdraws into distant fame.
He doesn't ever have to look at me again.

_____

In the aetherial or crystalline
morning, room floats
into the other
time. This is the act of writing
the only poem. The cat,
Wystan, likewise performs
The Cat. All my
curses and unpoetry here
as holy as the Bible or the future's
preferred broken page—
there's nothing wrong in this room.

_____

Blonde ferretface on Channel 3 announces
a bomb's exploded at St. Michel . . . many injured, a few dead . . .

no, it's just the anniversary of last year's bomb.
A scary trick of journalists . . . assholes.

_____

I'm back at school at night.
Columbia Campus on the Lower East Side
I run around its periphery, also systematically cut
into the center in diagonals, as fast as I can.
What's left to learn?
I still don't know enough to get out of this poem.

Something in another dream's a cloud of fluff or raffia:
I don't want to win that as knowledge,
just another book.

Yet this woman's book
this book on
near-death narratives is intelligent.
I believe the inside of these experiences
but not their figuration; what I
particularly hate about them is the parental
aspect of the Golden Light—always some-
one, something else doing the knowing and better loving, explaining
        what reality is.

———————————

"R-rose?" the boy says, promising to tell what he knows
of the mystical clothes. His lips seal over
into a smooth disc: a voice says for him, "Win my tip."
Soulgirl the little dark girl, presses the inside corners of her eyes
with thumb and forefinger. He's making her hysterical.
Then a 'grown woman' peeks under a dressing room curtain, says,
"I see you are the right." She has a big pocketbook.
This is called, in this version, the 'ing way anatobus'—
this is knowledge, my friends, that Mommy knows where
to peek at it, almost like Daddy, and later in time, in the postal time service
she'll really know, like him, and so, you too, little girl, will know.
The knowledge, flattered, says, "No, you shouldn'ta."

———————————

In Your Own Image:

Know the one truth in your own image.
It's still the truth.

———————————

Lashed in place, against a wall of rock, by a wide
black velvet band. Men want the cave in place and me in place,
        neither liberated,
so they can continue to discuss The Legacy Of, The Urgency Of . . .
their choice, *à volonté,* he says. Oysters at the Bistro Romain

# FURTHER FIGURATION OF MY REGRESSIVE BACKLASH

the famous songwriter/singer and I
are being coerced by a group of men
into having our genitals photographed—
in a plain room in morning light
we take off our pants and pose, casually,
he first, then he
sits on a toilet while I'm
being photographed. I guess
they're going to compare us, our un-
remarkable genitals. I'm flattered to be under
consideration (why am I like that?)
The famous songwriter/singer pays me no mind.

_____

The neon-green towers of the Las Vegas casinos,
just down the street from New York—how
can you live here? I say, to my friends, of this Everywhere.
Though I live, I mean leave, in Paris
writing of the deregulated green-money world
in continuous transition due to holy science/technology.

_____

. . . if TWA Flight 800
was shot down by a terrorist missile
one's more afraid to fly to or from Paris
than if it were a bomb . . .

Not *really* allowed to complain that all
existing power structures
are male. Because there's never
enough time for change
between bombs famines genocides—
You have to do something else

male right now! Don't stop, sit down
discuss the entire situation
from top to bottom with input from
every sort of person
both sexes; just do
the next forceful thing Now, Hurry, it's Urgent!

———————————————————

Last week's three rejection letters from men,
nothing to do with the fact that they're men.
None of this year's rejection letters, all from men have
anything to do with the fact that they're from men—not exactly—
has to do with what The Magazine wants. Which
has to do with the language of the various "dominant discourses," and
        neither
editorship nor discourse is a Male Structure?—must Prove that—
the burder of proof is always on One—
though all the editors so far involved have been men except for one who
        never answered—
and the "dominant discourses" still those invented by Donald Duck and
        Mickey Mouse:
Duck's being post-post-post quackery and Mouse's
the miming of excellent undergraduate papers circa 1965.

———————————————————

Can I afford this extra thing? a semi-transparent
tee-shirt? I choose a dark green one then change my mind I
look best in the black one so

grab it I'm about to go to occasion in big loft.

But I have to pee and my father's doing
something constructive in the bathroom;
I start to pee on the floor
he doesn't see though he finally
does let me in

I would have peed on the floor at the grownup
career occasion if I'd waited any longer! Because
I simply can't or won't

control myself anymore—it seems as if all I do
is pee on the floor.
So what about the not un-

gendered black
spiritual tee-shirt? Am I
going to wear it or not. (Pee isn't gendered.)

_____

My queer friend's destroyed and blackened face is getting better
after a lot of operations
he may be the keeper of the Grail
I like him but do I want his Grail—he's
such a bitch

        I escape

to a part of the house that I'm then
forbidden by women to enter
a sacred woman is in bed there, someone's
sacred cow as they say. I can't find
a room for myself. I've written this very
libretto
          Has some man written the score?
    . . . criticized
because it's too ragged, but it's what I say,
                   I say,
that's important. Because I'm in court in the witness
box and I want to insult the judge. So I can find
my own so-called Grail . . .

_____

Well these important texts are all about sheep
they're layered and broken up, so sophisticated
this dream: first we see a monolithic block,
an impressive unified text; then
it breaks up into two parallel columns and they're
impressive too, avant-garde
                 Katharine Hepburn's
quavery voice says, "Baaah! Baaah!"

In our rough math
spooky texture
of stars seems known . . .

That building, the building
of knowing the stars, is too high
in order
to keep people in
their place
under a sulphur sky

# DON'T THINK THAT THOUGHT IT WILL POISON THIS MOMENT

"what ribbon are you?
As a rhythm talks you,
you are one . . . "

said a voice, in my head
last night.

_____

I go into a woman's room of dark wood.
She's lying on her four-poster, reading a magazine.
She says, in her casual way, "Oh for
instance her head is there, there, there . . ."
She points to the wall; I see no head but sense
stratifications in the wall. These aren't
marks of growth but indicate layers of burials of
actual heads—the same head? I'm afraid I'll see it . . . Instead
what I thought were windows turn out to be
dioramas of men, 17th Century cavaliers, who
come to life and begin to struggle over us,
over whether or not they can "have" us. Some
of the men support our freedom, some don't:
whatever they support, it seems to be _their_ fight.

_____

What kind of life is this?
_The_ life, and yet not mine
it's always someone else's . . .

it belongs to the other guy on the panel
of fellow experts. You know who. Wait
ten more years
Anyone but oneself.

That's what "postmodern" means
that with this theory of
diverse voices, the predictable man
holds power.

He knows the "web of signs" real well.
What can you know that he doesn't?

———————————————

Spiritual means inviolable
in this moment. You can't get
next to me—I can forgive
by floating away. Because
some things are unforgivable, but
it's much worse for me than for you.
You will never fathom your crime. I
will know I can't forgive it. All established
religions fail at this point,
all previously articulated practice of the spiritual.

As does politics:
the longer change takes, the more
there is to forgive.
Until one has no interest in forgiveness.

———————————————

It's official that National Front skinheads
violated the Jewish cemetery
in Carpentras. Le Penis
will address the situation tonight, which he's
currently calling "bizarre." More free
publicity. He needs some. Tall black women
are winning Olympic medals for France,
shrieking with joy.

———————————————

A black man—who?—face covered with soil
lies next to me in the cemetery. No
we're in bed together, now, sheets with soil on them . . .

What do I know on my own?
a hot illusion, a house and car
oppress all but their manufacturers. Though
other people seem to be on terms with
what possesses them.

And so and so has the
answer,
even in my dreams two nights ago—
refer it to Him. He understands the chains of
our illusions. Of course he does he's
one of their manufacturers

He invented me, being a He, that's how he got to be Guru.

So start, myself, start, where. Before
anyone invented me. This very minute . . .
no time to complain or forgive.

It's all alone, the Everything.
Alone's no condition, it's a word.
A beaut, a real beaut.
How alone can I be.
Someone climbs their own stairs
in the middle of my transparency.
In the middle of me.

Climb up the sacred wire to heaven,
the sky's full of shamans flying.
Or stay right here with no one, me.
I'm staying here.

The Devil is so white you can't see his features.
He dresses in dark suit and tie
He asserts he'll take me to lunch. My
friend and I find out we work for him,
in arts administration. He dresses us:

I'm Cleopatra; my friend is pregnant, she
has to wait for her true outfit. So I'm pasting
temporary decorations on her loose-fitting dress.
A picture of white fur won't do. I settle
on a cartoon depiction of a little girl's hand reaching
out to grab hold of her mother's dress,
tropical sunset in background . . . our version of Adam and God.
All this takes place because I've come down,
come down from the top story of a big house, at night.
In this dream outside's daylight, inside's always night.
I work for the Devil. I will "die in a monument,
like Cleopatra." Who cares. But I can't undo
my life so far, of trying to unlock the male secret
of poetic form, the Devil's secret.
Now I know it better than you do, than practically
any you. do I still want it. or anything.
Or change to what. I will never live, the white
Devil sees to that. He comes to all my parties;
I welcome him because I'm equalitarian.
I'll ride in a car with anyone and flash
my Cleopatra décolletage, just to see if it works.

———————————————

What ribbon are you? I enter the atmosphere of heavel,
hovel of heaven, in a second. I do keep
doing that too, it's part of my ribbon

that comes roaring out of the lion's mouth

## THE LONGEST VAMPIRIC HISTORY VS. THE SOUL

this man in a dugout, middle of Front Street
near where the trains come in,
presents me with evidence that men love me—
a letter from a tragically dead gay poet containing
color sketches of me young and longhaired—
so that the 'lions' beside me can be mollified.
I'm giving in to vanity, as the man says from
his trench, "Everyone loves you." He will never
budge from his protective wartime position.

———————————————

I'm worn
from trying to integrate
'dreams' and 'life . . .'
my temper
dominates me a frightful sub-
terranean energy—
lion—doesn't respond to
affection. Wilder
than that
wilder than wiles.

———————————————

Every night, it seems, I go to an open store
to sleep in a back room. Ashamed of my housedress,
urine-stained. One night I aid a woman there
and am praised for it by another.
Otherwise, the non-story continues . . .

the air in the lines between sections enclosing,
among other things,
motions from room to room . . .

a figure of self-doubt shakes but doesn't topple.
It could scream: she, I, could scream, wouldn't die.
Could say a lot of hurtful things, into the sky or onto
the page, wouldn't die. The addressees
wouldn't die, either. So what's all this shit about "words?"

---

On top of an Alp, in a crow's nest,
with figure of Hardwood. He's
performing gymnastic feats, on the bars
of our little railing, just over infinity.
The will is basically a showoff. I
don't think he'll fall; what's more likely,
in this kind of situation, he'll
knock our pouch of papers into
the abyss. Lose my poem.

---

The petals of the August lotus have opened at
the Jardin des Plantes, the lotus being
in the special fenced-off section.
Why fenced off? It isn't Ours. Except
during certain Hours.

---

In the House of Meditation, down here among my bones
it's mollusk-pink; ideas and dreams
begin here. Some line up, four pearls, a single voice speaks:
"We have seen it in your corridors, in your body: that grace
is an adhesion to the cliffs of tissue inside you,
dissolves into clouds and follows its own route through.
What we're telling you is that it's physical. Corrigible mapways.
Fix the ring where the path or wrath flows.
The way is a flow,
dissolves barrier levels
of phosphorescent calcifications—and then
there's a door, in a body wall, through which a voice is released . . ."

I realize that above the earth there are folds of air tissue
similar to the folds of flesh inside me.

I realize that in death
I will be a voice that doesn't speak. Doesn't have to speak.

---

Another one of Those Dreams. He's
a handsome moustached Latino this time;
he comes on to me in a bank. Standing,
by accident, on the other side of the table, as we
scrawl on our pieces of paper, he soon shows me he has,
by accident, filled out a withdrawal slip for my account.
It looks like one of my handwritten poems. That's
how I know he loves me. The next thing's a competition,
which I watch not compete in. He
parks his car on the special mound for competitors,
gets out agitatedly, zipping his fly: everyone enters
the Club; where he wins with a song accompanied by guitar
and two backup voices. The Father and the Holy Ghost no doubt.

---

Voice:
"People say you've got a lot of trouble
over the year.

Lost accident, a music lesson
bad for the woman.
I don't want to make you scream again in company,
but—"

Then a scar crawls over a cylinder of light. Onto a stage.
The scar is a snappy tuner, and says:
"Fuck 'em up! Our crowd tonight!
It's still my turn to sing."
The star-shaped scar then screams:

"Ribald Rheinhart, I love you
. . . You saaavvvee
my liiife
a-gain!"

The man I really love doesn't
save my life. Who'd want such bullshit

he steals us clothes to wear
when we arrive naked
in the parking lot of our new casino
or country. Another man rushes up
to me with a tea-holder spoon, snapping it
open and closed. He says, "I hate it
when feminists talk like this"

# PLEASE DON'T ANYONE SAVE MY LIFE PASSIM

will achieve a
stripped aloneness that
can flood back out.
Stripped of world stuff

that's why I have to help repaint the town hall.
My mother has painted a tree on the wall of
one ground-floor room but
a horrible woman keeps doctoring it—worse each time.
She has a trick I hate, a computer-image-type tree
gets produced from a brush in a moment.
So I go downstairs; where I'm now painting a wall as blank as I can.
Famous men are around down here.
They turn out to be small and thin-chested
in love or importantly sequestered, the little shits.

Is anything changed enough yet? Can I leave this poem?

———————————————

Smell of cat piss.
Healthy.
Get rid of everything except
for the green coverlet, smell
of piss, starlings yelling.

I do that
by myself.

———————————————

The dream never really got started
last night because I left my apartment
in uptown New York for the movie theaters
too late. I couldn't find a movie (read "dream")
I wanted to enter. One was ancient Egyptian in theme

(read "dead" for "ancient Egyptian") from 1967,
a sphinx on the marquee, a tale of
white aliens, burrowing underground like termites (read
staking out my unconscious for their own uses
cheap little conquerors), directed by Stanley ("Strangelove") Kubrick
(read disappearance of a civilization: all ours or my
personal one before 1967 the year I
graduated from college, thoroughly burrowed and ready for
the further fucking) . . .

So I couldn't find a dream I wanted to be in. They were all
old pharaonic hat. Old woes

perhaps I am
emptying out.

But nothing can be done without some imagery.

———————————————

That's another room, right in the wall.
Right in the interstices.
It's empty, old.
No one moves in, worn linoleum.
Sit down.
I don't need a better room right now.

———————————————

red worlds yellow sky a hell

have doll's stiff arms to be slammed, by what,
repeatedly against red rock, my back against rock.
Yellow over hellmouth
indentation between peaks. My back
has been strengthened.

slip of a man slip of a man, world
is a slip of a man—it
rode you like a horse, looks so natural.
Told you to think like a hatchet or
not think. Told you to think. Well

that kind of thinking's for warlocks. Abjure
every single responsibility, to start.

eyes are helpless in the raw state.
Can't handle looking at nothing
Pull self back from a dress, look at that.

he was in bed with her I walked in
and screamed at him, an old dream of what
never happened. And isn't about him. The
deeper meaning of faithlessness
is that a civilization has it,
redeyed, repulsive.

Cheap fucks, so one can be a star
in the small world—
'He's fucked more kinds of knowledge than anyone I know.'
They were creep Zodiac, all those ages of knowing:
I've been sick, playing along for the last fifty years.

---

Look at empty blank wall . . .
repainted an already yellowed cream
and the worn grey floor has been dripped on somewhat.
What's looking

. . . and a dark maw opens to the left
a left hand opens with a dark blotch on it

that was the door that led here.

Mitch, Souldark, a story.
Now it's stopped being a story.

The pod of a spaceship opens vagina-like
to show its fig newton insides.
You love that. You think
I'm being typical, to say that and not
something You'd say which
You'd consider a very surprising revelation.

Alien gave me steel hand to clasp.
I told it go away I'm the alien.

Don't need the ship image don't need the fig image

just need in my head the interstitial room

# LION

graduated from spiritual high school last night;
from a house on the outskirts of Paris where
we'd had glasses of champagne,
"kids" went off in two groups to party—except
some returned secretly to the house, its champagne.
I got separated from everyone, hunted futilely for our
two—female and male—"authority figures."
Then, searched for a bar, but behind University Place,
on an alley named after World Stuff, named after "jazz."
I woke up and peed; went back to sleep. Suddenly
the male authority figure was sexily saying goodbye to me,
the morning after the party. Then I was chatting with the female one,
via walkie-talkie, in a large hotel lobby. When she
saw me I ran away. Finally the address of the house
where last night began has been posted: the house
is on a street named for a cove. Laguna Street. But
laguna's also lacuna—a space between official places.
I haven't been conscious during all of my progress.
Laguna Street previously existed in the space between sections.

---

Seem to be in "the room in the wall."

Sit. On the empty floor legs in front of me.
Washed desert light in here (though Paris is grey).
It's just like Needles in here, spring in the desert, air of, light of.

---

The food served at the next party was cooked plants with thick stalks.
The preparation took place in a kitchen on the Golden Gate Bridge, at night.
The outfit that Wisdom wore to the party was a big, vulgar, plumed hat
and a red and black flared dress. The party's already over. I
hate that. I sat next to a dead old friend
his awkward body, his nervous smile. I didn't want to sleep with him.

I didn't get enough to drink, am pouring myself a
white wine, pouring it into successively smaller glasses.
That's because I have to keep cutting this poem.
Frankly I'm not sure the whole meal has been served yet.

---

A voice says, as I'm falling asleep,
"I'm working on the circulation, where the dark is fundamental."

---

Patrick Poivre D'Arvor
is going to sail from
Québec to Bretagne. Thinking
it over, he says. With several sailors.
Their intelligent, brainy arms
work the ropes, hoisting the sails.

---

repeat: To start again I have to be nothing.

---

I seem to be at a University
It has filthy toilets shit-barnacled
And outside in the big hallway I see
A lot of incomplete people
Many of them are just heads on rollers
Many of the heads are statuary—prosthetic
Heads containing, presumably,
At least portions of the organ.

---

Sit and nothing to say. Please don't try
to do something to me—even while I'm
sitting here—the way You all do. The way
You do it from a distance.

. . . Because I work on my poem all night in my dreams I'm
always tired.
"What does the word 'desire' suggest to you?" "A corny movie."
I suppose it was a beautiful movie. Fuck that.

. . . A dog dressed as a woman.
Arf is wearing a calico bonnet.
Because I've been trying to enter Your world, on Your terms, for a long time.

The shoes are on the floor upsidedown:
a whole person's up there in high heels
walking on the ceiling upsidedown.
You could turn the world over, so she's rightsideup
and You're upsidedown. After these thousands of years
You could for a while.

———————————————

The roar of a lion.
The empty room
in the wall is filled with a roar
like air but not like air
and certainly not like sound it's filling
my ears like golden yellow saturated
soundlessness until I could explode.

———————————————

The radical poets, that
male lense. They wore trinitarian goggles:
lens for eye, lens for eye, lens for mouth:
Western Christian (Father, Son, and
Holy Absence) denouncing patriarchy patriarchally.
Women loved it, the stupid sluts.
Liberated by party bosses into their own discourses.
"We have freed our slaves," a man says.
The women are fixing up their own apartment.
They're using the vocabulary which according to the men
will serve their purposes best. They explain this, then
one woman says to me, ". . . especially you—
your self-reflexivity's
an insult to my property . . .
your poem takes us back two whole centuries . . ."
Well! That's very abacal of her—abracadabracal?

Nothing must ever be said.
You must never say it.
Language is exactly for not speaking.
There are many learned ways of not speaking.

everywhere I
turn, my *intelligence* is denied
except
in the roaring air where I deny You

eating my
meal, which is possibly
You,
like a lion

# A NEW HAIRDO

I stand at the docks before immense ocean liners
and tell two relevant officials I'm re-entering
the country illegally. They say that's fine.
I find the man I've travelled with and tell him
that of the three things we've brought, he
can have the two wooden crates
and I'll take the third thing, which is darkness and leeks.
This must mean I'm Ereshkigal not
Inanna, the Underworld not Earth and Heaven,
hair of writhing leeks, in labor with what child . . . oh
only this ridiculous poem I suppose.
The man later joins me in a house so I can
teach him the Cobra posture. I seem to be
all snakes in this dream; in which we later make jokes of
a Republican senator's most serious pronouncement—
he's appearing in the frames of a comic strip, pontificating against,
I believe, immigration. That's me.
What a joke. You can't keep the Queen of Hell out—
no stupid Christian cracker can . . .

---

Someone's child, now dead, was so deformed
does she wonder if the girl should have
been born. No, she rarely thinks like that
since the child was. Was was . . . a life
not an ethical question; the question
of abortion is a head trip, a place a
cell of static projection, non-life
the discussion is a dead dead place. center zero.
Both sides in an abortion debate are dead. As
someone's dead deformed child is still curiously alive.

In the interstices . . .
What do I know now
Know isn't the word—

Beginning from a single point of
not knowing what You know,
I don't choose any of Your studies.
except a hint of metrics

Close eyes, burrow into body.
Tell me a thing to say, body

"No origin. Not like."

Rule now: a careful emptiness.

---

The heroine of the dream is a junkie
young girl. It's a secret.
Outside the party in the dark with her addict lover—
they're in a conspiratorial, warm embrace.
He says, "Do you want a glass of wine or some heroin?"
She laughs meaningfully . . .

Get rid of them.

Only a dark street in Bagnolet
only the street in the banlieu is left,
only the street itself. And somewhere
docks with huge prows of freighters

Keep the ships
keep the ships in my images.

---

All the *sans papiers,* the illegal immigrants, Africans
who've been holed up in St. Bernard Church
for weeks, on hunger strike
until they receive legal papers, will be forced out today

for deportation. They laid in the church last night,
in blue sleeping bags, receiving visitors.
Sit up briefly, shake hands, lie back down.

---

Ereshkigal, naked, hair of leeks:
Keep her.

---

Drink this salt, You.
You are the cause of my pain.
You aren't I.
I can't kill You. Why?
Because there would be no life. And because
Your death hurts me.
I won't go any further than that.
This is a start. And that
in the room in the wall, I can barely know You.
Outside it, I'm serenely wary.

This is the beginning of a new
spiritual and ethical position. For a woman.
Based on the supposition of harmful intent—
that another, male or female, even without realizing it
might very well want to hurt me, cause my subjugation.
I don't propose an equalitarian lovingkindness or compassion.
I propose, for women, always an instinctive wariness.
I propose, further, meditation in separate closets, without
instructions. That's
the whole religion. It never has to be proposed again
in order to exist. It has no organization and no beliefs.

---

A many-armed god
seizes me from behind
and crushes
broken glass into my face—
the Grail?
He says, "You've just earned
10,000 years of ignorance!"

He crushes more glass into
my face, "10,000 years of torture!"

---

The college kids cheer on
the couple fucking onscreen,
while in a side room, a girl's room,
I look for underpants to steal.
I need them and some creme rinse.
Then I need to get out of here

# THE CHAPLET ON THE DONKEY'S HEAD:
## BOTH KEEP DISSOLVING


if you never quite let it be a poem
you might write one
but
there are a lot
of other
ways.

        Writing a poem, I
construct a magenta fan
with a photolikeness, enclosed in a central oval,
of a beloved relation, with her hair brown
that is not to say, before her hair turned grey:
it's her essential self.

Someone's jealous of the attention
I'm paying her in my work
because he wants it all for his art
which is a pure, gridded, layer of words
painted in crosshatched grey monochrome brushstrokes.
Your art, he seems to say to me, kisses life's ass.
His art asks that his own ass be kissed.

        ——————————————

There's a stove in the recesses of the room in the wall.

Deliciously steamy weather . . . I'm embroiled
in one of my tortured perimenopausal pre-periods:
cramps, depression, dizziness, moaning,
foreboding: I enjoy this for its transient
intensity; often accompanied by
poetic or philosophical insight.

Among seaside cliffs in South America,
it was a question of lifting someone's—Mark's—
ornate cabinet, shaped like a cathedral organ,
full of all his possessions—lifting it from the lagoon,
via helicopter, and conveying it to his new house somewhere.
Wouldn't it, I reflected, be possible to deposit
the cabinet directly into the house, through an
attic window or even the ceiling itself? After all,
this is a dream. No, I decided,
the cabinet must be lowered next to the house
and his things carried inside the house one by one.

I must be the man, Mark; oh as usual
I'm the man too. I'm Patsy
calling out that I'm a dupe, a stupid
usee, victim of a huge social ripoff
an ordinary piece of meat, with a
limp salami hanging down in this heat.

If I could just get all of myself into my house.

In Belgium a creep who'd raped several children
was let out of prison after three years, for good conduct.
He's been systematically kidnapping young and also older girls,
the occasional boy. Has had assistants—one of whom, he says,
allowed two eight-year-old girls to starve to death
in a locked room. He says he murdered that man for that.
Two missing teenage girls may have been sold off abroad
as prostitutes, can't be found. The kids are used
for pornography as well as prostitution and the pimps' gratification . . .

somehow different from the "normal" world
of pornography and prostitution?
Because there are families who care about the victims or something.
           That mess
of a whore at the foot of Montmartre
selling herself to ugly old men in the neighborhood—
not like *those* little girls, no one's ever wanted her back.

Having survived, she can now be accused
of being partly responsible for the fact
that society needs whores. Needs
little girls to get fucked in photos, in order to promulgate
civil libertarian values, the right of a man
to whack off to his favorite fantasy.

———————————————

I can't get this dream, I said in it. I
can't get it, what should I remember? I can't
      even find it . . .
Someone said, It's right here, it's what you
      just saw, right?

Two identical invisible entities, with sort of wire coils . . .
a woman's, a man's, soul.

———————————————

The body is not an eye or any other of its parts
or the totality of them
it isn't anything at all as itself. And
the person cannot be measured as a "what it is,"
a "who she is," etc. When
you measure me, I'm measuring you:
there's no one outside us.
           We love each other
in that love refers to intimate relation:
our species always intimate with itself,
loving it, loving it to death. We are
more than that, more than a species. Any one of us
is the one ground of life,
the only true point-of-view.
We are each unique too, self-bounded in no way that
can be defined or measured

# THE ONE THOUSAND ARMS OF POKING AND PINCHING LOVE

try to remember
a shadowy world
of a stripper.
She walked and talked all
night, wearing a dress
keeping it on. I my-
self still watching and
waiting for further
disclosures, insights
Demi Moore, nearly moored.

---

The blood-black dahlias blooming
on the foreheads of all the sapped corpses
in last night's movie—

saw them at the Jardin yesterday.
Also a pale wrinkled moon
of a hibiscus,
some scarlet waterlilies

nothing's happening
in deep August. Except for
silent openings.

---

I will take my anti-matter
anti-matter and singling,
wrapped up in a ghost
take that away.
                    'Song)
when I die.

Will wash my leeks this morn
in Palmolive Shampoo.

---

Death to all evangels,
death to the head of state
death to monsieur's rhetoric,
death to us all!

Death to your pitiful salary
death to your obnoxious blonde beauty
death to your piety, intelligence
your efforts on behalf of your people;
death to your delicate feelings
death to your honor, death to your anarchy
death to your ancient customs, your
lovely usages; your criminality;
death to your goodness
death to all your mystiques.

---

Inside a mound with a man at night
in a dark misty field of such mounds.
Haven't we been here before? Of course.
And really, there's nothing to fear from the ghosts—
are we the ghosts?—there's
nothing to fear at any rate; there
should never have been anything to fear.
Evolutionist, there should have been no fear
no sorrow . . .

Later, I'm no longer dead in a mound; I'm
alive again in a large social house
which still has an upper story
and a rosette of trenches on the first floor.
It contains, as well, a fat spiritual presence.
Should the soul eat quite so many
chocolates, oh why not? A more
serious problem is how can it fuck its
lover, with all these people around on the

first floor entrenched . . . always
about their business right in the house!

---

When to end—
ending itself will tell me. It always does.
Maybe not in this poem, maybe the next.

---

A lot of pushing
elbowing, poking. The nicest
people do it all the time;
getting you to be good
like them.
Then, sometimes they cry
when you're not.

                  I've taken some
care that this poem not be a nice place.

. . . nothing to keep one from an
internal freedom
which lifts the person off the whole
globe and its sleazy little continents—

leave the damn place for a while, anytime you want.

---

You are a lovely man (you,
not you). A crystal set,
a prick, a coincident entirety.

---

I'm being served more chocolate for dessert
tamales with mole sauce
pieces of chocolate hidden in the filling.

While I eat, my companions evince
their problematical natures.
This woman shouts that she's going to have

an operation and an abortion.
This man is very tall, keeps growing taller.

I'm interested, I am, but I eat my chocolate.
She's being served some too—
take it and eat it, you fuckhead;
as far as I can tell, what we're here for,
to scarf up soul goo. You pay for it too,
pay for each course: pay each other to live—
why?—obviously because we're such creeps.
That nice lady there makes me pay her:
she makes me tell her I love her over and over.
Just eat, I want to say, there's plenty of chocolate

a cognac-soaked cherry slides down my throat

# THE USUAL AND THE MOST TENUOUS OF GOODBYES

we're auditioning this week, an old lady and others
and I still auditioning for a man, a figure of
the Will though he isn't Hardwood.
We're all in toilet stalls peeing, because
that's what you do before you try out
for the part, get rid of yourself
                                    I'm
auditioning for leaving my poem.
Auditioning for stupid recognition. Aren't I always?

I figure I haven't been doing too well
this week, have made a drab presentation
previously to this director, dispenser of rewards.
All of us women file out of the toilets
towards his office, to try for the part . . . I
don't want to be a part,
a medieval idea, a veritable
stay-in-your-place idea.
A very modern idea, like working for Bill Gates, work

for a man. Save your money.

————————————————

The French government will review the cases
of the *sans papiers* one by one. Many
will undoubtedly be sent back.
I won't ever be sent back, I have a gift
for obtaining *papiers:* I'm white.
I've often used this talent worthily,
e.g. for walking around unharassed by
the cops of international capitals.
Was often harassed by men of various
races when younger, but rarely by official
authorities, keepers of *papiers*

Good luck on your auditions,
*mesdames et messieurs sans papiers.*

———————————————

Why do I live here. Why not
That's not a good enough reason
I'm giving up on reasons.

———————————————

Voice: "Is that bump in any language?"
Voice: ". . . deformed image . . . it is self-contained."
Must be a poem.

———————————————

. . . something unexpected, full of foul humor.

As well as a ribbon,
a roar, a grace, a dialogue, a diary,
and an individual
act of disobedience, defiance of
whoever comes to mind

I can't keep writing
can hardly remember my dreams now

Have I fed anyone.
Have I changed Your image of what a poem might be
and so, in some part, changed "reality."

———————————————

Monday morning, jackhammers

then in the interstitial space
between interior dark and matter-of-fact light
if I open the windows in either wall, can day and night blend.
A strange, a tossing ghostly seawater effect
in which I'm enveloped, just sitting
drowning in it . . .

They call your work "engaging" when
A) you're a woman
        and
B) it doesn't conform to prescribed
models of pomposity or obfuscation
rather, "talks."

"Engaging" is an asshole word,
not quite as obnoxious a cliché as "ground-breaking."

---

The little girl in the big house, Angie,
is still in trouble. A rose will save her
a heavy, heavy rose—her life lived will save
her. If she can just live it.
This rose, heavy to carry but light to see,
heavy to live through petal by petal, in sequence,
but light to be, all at once. Save her from our ideas
which rip the rose into pieces. The tyrant of our mind
encircles her with a rich white house instead of
a rose of any color: red-black, apricot, blue . . .

---

I rescue the little boy from the pedophiles on Front Street
their maze of rooms between the former drugstore and the former jewelers.
Because no one knows what a child is: himself,
not a part in a personal fantasy. Did
You ever know who I was as a child? Never—
A part in society's fantasy, as far as You were concerned . . .
The roof is sinking.
It's very close to the top of my head, roof of the jewelers but
we've escaped and don't have to wear
the crucial rings of obedience.

---

. . . we're told we behave in accordance with
our bodies, our so-called genes. Well, we're not
trapped by our "makeup"

we're trapped by Your supposed naming and mastery of it.
You then make us wear Your makeup.

---

The famous musician/songwriter and I
are a dream team again.
He's wearing both a dress and pants.
We're hiding together, away from
the dusty Western street
where the saddest song of the film
must be sung. But if that death song filled
the present, as it does,
we would be in heaven, he and I, in the dust.

---

I've found a peaceful circular ride
in an amusement park at night
I could ride it forever

Alice Notley was born in Bisbee, Arizona, on November 8, 1945, and grew up in Needles, California. She was educated at Barnard College and at The Writers Workshop, University of Iowa, receiving the appropriate degrees. During the late sixties and early seventies she lived a peripatetic, rather outlawish poet's life (San Francisco, Bolinas, London, Essex, Chicago) before settling on New York's Lower East Side. For sixteen years there, she was an important force in the eclectic second generation of the so-called New York School of poetry. She has never tried to be anything but a poet, and all her ancillary activities have been directed to that end. She is the author of more than twenty books of poetry, including *At Night the States*, the double volume *Close to Me and Closer . . . (The Language of Heaven)* and *Désamère*, and *How Spring Comes*, which was a winner of the San Francisco Poetry Award. Her *Selected Poems* was published in 1993. Her book-length poem *The Descent of Alette* was published by Penguin in 1996, followed by *Mysteries of Small Houses* (1998), which was one of three nominees for the Pulitzer Prize and was the winner of the *Los Angeles Times* Book Award for Poetry. She is a two-time NEA grant recipient and the recipient of a General Electric Foundation Award, a NYFA fellowship, several awards from The Fund for Poetry, and a grant from the Foundation for Contemporary Performance Arts, Inc. In April of 2001, Notley received The Shelley Memorial Award from the Poetry Society of America, and in May of 2001 she received an Academy Award in Literature from the Academy of Arts and Letters. She now lives permanently in Paris.

Printed in the United States
by Baker & Taylor Publisher Services